I0541947

Malt Liquor
to
Holy Water

Overcoming the Malt Liquor Trap of '93

STACY MARTIN

Copyright © 2024 by Stacy Martin

All rights reserved.

Disclaimer

I am not your personal counselor. The information shared in this book is based on my observations, knowledge, and personal experience. I offer this as a testimony of my journey, in the hope that it might inspire and guide you on your own path.

Isaiah 65:24 (KJV):

*"And it shall come to pass, that before they call,
I will answer; and while they are yet speaking, I will hear."*

Table of Contents

Introduction

***

The Journey from the Streets to the Unseen

Back in the early 90s, it felt like the world was pushing us in one direction. **Gangsta rap** and **malt liquor** weren't just part of the culture—they were the culture. We didn't question it. Snoop dropped **The Chronic**, and suddenly, we were all drinking 40s and acting like tomorrow didn't matter. The streets had a script, and we followed it without even thinking. It was all about being hard, living reckless, and ignoring the fact that we were being set up to fail.

But as I grew older, I realized there was something behind the music, the culture, and the image they sold us. They wanted us trapped—trapped in addiction, trapped in cycles of violence, and trapped in a system designed to keep us down. And I got caught in it, just like so many others. For years, I was stuck in that cycle—drinking, pretending, and ignoring the emptiness growing inside of me.

But this isn't just a story about my fall. This is about the **rise**, the climb back up, and how I found my way out through **faith**. And here's the real twist—this journey isn't just about what we can see or touch. It goes deeper than that. Way deeper.

I'm gonna take you from the streets of **North Philly** into a world most of us never think about—a world that's been there all along. **Quantum physics**, **metaphysics**, and **scripture** all play a role in this journey. Yeah, we're going there. I'm talking about **faith** not just as something you believe in, but something that's as real as the streets we grew up on. You see, science is just starting to prove what the Bible's been telling us all along—that the world we see is just a small part of the bigger picture.

This book is my story—how I went from drowning in malt liquor and gangsta culture to finding **God's grace** and uncovering the truth about how this world really works. It's not just about recovery—it's about **transformation** on every level. And the best part? The same power that saved me is available to you.

Section 1

MY STORY

Chapter 1

✦

The Early Days - Discovering Alcohol

1993 was the year everything changed for me. I was just 16, but I thought I had it all figured out. My boys and I went to see *Menace II Society*—that movie was everything we thought life should be. Carjacking, gangbanging, drinking 40s on the corner—it was like a blueprint for how to be a real one. We walked out of that theater hyped, ready to live that life.

Back then, I was rocking my signature look—white tees, Timberland boots, and a Jesus piece chain. My nickname was **Juice-DaMac**. It was at a hotel party when Snoop Dogg's "Ain't No Fun" came on, and I took the lyrics literally: "It ain't no fun if the homies can't have none." It became a part of my identity, and the crew started calling me JuiceDaMac after that night.

It really felt like the good old days. **Philly summers were hot, and the streets were alive with cookouts, block parties, and late-night corner sessions**. The scent of BBQ and the sound of ice-cream truck music filled the air, while everyone acted like they had no worries. We'd be posted up by the street phone like it was our throne, waiting for the next call or just hanging around, acting like we ran the block. I was too young to understand the full weight of what we were getting into back then—too caught up in the high of it all. But looking back, I see it for what it was: **a trap**. While some people moved on, some of us stayed stuck, not realizing how deep we were in.

That night after *Menace II Society*, we hit up the corner store. Each of us chipped in to grab a couple of 40s—that was the thing back then, **40-ounce bottles of malt liquor**. We called them "40s," "Snaps," "Petro," and they were like a badge of honor. The corner was our throne, and those bottles were our crown.

We cracked them open right there on the street, passing them around like we owned the night. When it was my turn, I took a long swig. The cold, bitter liquid went down hard, but I loved the way it made me feel. **It was like a wave hit me—washing away all my insecurities, my fears, my doubts**. For the first time, I felt invincible. The alcohol was more than just a drink—it was an escape.

That night, we roamed the streets, feeling untouchable. We laughed, we talked trash, and we acted like we ran the city. The **40s gave us a false sense of confidence**, making us feel like we were more than we were. But looking back now, yeah it was just—a trap. The more I drank, the more I needed that feeling. What started as something fun quickly turned into a habit, then a necessity. And just like that, I was hooked.

Chapter 2

---❉---

The Grip of Addiction

By 1995, I was deep into the game. I had reconnected with a girl I'd met at a block party in '93—Precious. She was different from the other girls I knew—down-to-earth, family-oriented, even at a young age. There was something special about her, and I could sense it from the start. We had our first daughter, Stacey, in '96, and I should have been clear about the direction I needed to lead my family. I loved the feeling of becoming a father and cherished every moment of my kids being born. But beneath the joy, there was a growing sense of uncertainty.

Even though I loved my kids, I was torn between two worlds—**the life I wanted and the one I was already deep in**. Alcohol had me caught up. By the time our second child, Sadyrah, was born in '98, it was getting harder to balance it all. I'd come home late, smelling like liquor, feeling guilty but not guilty enough to stop. By 2001, when our third child, Sianni, was born, the cracks in my life were showing.

Precious could see it too. She noticed the way I'd drift off mentally, even when I was home. She noticed the **way alcohol was pulling me further away,** like a chain tightening every time I took another drink. I wanted to be a better man for my family, but the bottle kept calling my name.

Chapter 3

The Wake-Up Call – Falling, Rising, and Starting Over

By the time 2020 rolled around, the world was hit with the COVID-19 pandemic, and everything slowed down. It was like the whole city came to a halt. I had been out of the streets for years, but during the lockdown, I was faced with a different kind of battle—**the one inside me. Alcohol had taken its toll** over the years, and now, in this isolation, it felt like all the demons I'd been running from finally caught up with me.

Social isolation wasn't new for me. Even before the pandemic, I had been withdrawing more and more. **Anxiety and depression** became my constant companions, and alcohol was the only thing that seemed to keep them at bay. But during the pandemic, when the world shut down, I realized how much I had been relying on the bottle to keep me going. It was no longer about fun or escape—it was about survival.

For the first time since I started drinking, I managed to stop for a while. Six months sober. I thought maybe I had this thing beat. It felt like a fresh start, like I could finally leave all the years of drinking behind me. But then the holidays came around, and like so many others, I let my guard down. It was supposed to be just one drink—just one. But that **one drink turned into a disaster**.

Before I knew it, I was back where I started, drinking like I hadn't been sober for a single day. It was as if I had invited my demons back, and this time they brought company. **Matthew 12:45 (KJV)** warns, *"Then goeth he, and taketh with himself seven other spirits more wicked than himself, and they enter in and dwell there: and the last state of that man is worse than the first."* That's exactly what happened. I wasn't just drinking—I was losing myself all over again.

I was out of my head, acting a fool, spiraling back into the same cycle. It was clear I hadn't learned a damn thing. **Proverbs 26:11 (KJV)** says, *"As a dog returneth to his vomit, so a fool returneth to his folly."* That was me—foolish and lost.

Precious had enough. She gave me an ultimatum—either I get my act together, or she was moving on without me. That shook me to my core. For the first time, I saw how close I was to losing every-thing. Not just my family, but my future, my purpose—everything I had been fighting for. **I thought to myself, I'm about to go out like a loser.**

A few weeks later, on January 12, 2021, I finally quit drinking for good. But this time, I knew I couldn't do it on my own. I had tried before and failed. This time, I had to reach out to someone bigger than myself. I prayed hard, asking **Jesus** to deliver me from this addiction. I asked Him to either save me or save my family from me. It was in that moment of surrender that things started to change.

Chapter 4

Finding Faith – When Everything Else Falls Apart

I'm not going to sugarcoat anything—it wasn't easy. When I made the decision to quit drinking for good, I knew I needed something stronger than my own willpower. I had tried to do it on my own before, and every time I failed. This time, I needed something bigger, something more solid to hold onto. That's when I turned to faith.

My journey with faith didn't start in 2021, though. **It started way back in 2009,** long before I had fully committed to getting sober. One night, I was scrolling through YouTube on my PlayStation, literally right after asking God for a sign, and I found just that. I stumbled across a sermon by **Pastor Michael Hoggard**, and at first, I didn't think much of it. He was talking about the significance of numbers in the Bible—how every number had a meaning and a purpose.

At first, it just seemed like another preacher trying to make connections where there were none. But the more I listened, the more it all started to click. **Pastor Mike** showed how **every number in the Bible** was connected to something deeper, like God was using these numbers to show us that His Word wasn't random—it was woven together with precision. That's when I realized the Bible wasn't just a book—it was **the inspired Word of God**. That hit me hard.

Even though I didn't fully embrace faith at that moment, it planted a seed in me. It was the first time I started to see that there was more to life than just what I was living. But like so many other things, that realization got lost in the shuffle. **I was still caught up in the drinking**, in the lifestyle, and while I wanted to be more connected to God, the bottle kept pulling me back.

Over the years, I kept coming back to faith, but it was always half-hearted. **I even got involved with Pastor Mike's Bethel Church Facebook group**, trying to stay plugged in. At one point, I even became an admin in the group, helping manage posts and keep the community running. But all the while, I was still drinking. I was living a double life—wanting to be a man of faith, but still trapped in the old habits. **In 2019**, I finally stepped down from my role as admin because I knew I couldn't keep pretending like I had it all together.

Still, I never fully let go of faith. Even at my lowest, I held onto it like a lifeline, something I could turn to when I was ready. **By 2021**, after the wake-up call, I knew it was time to finally lean into it. I couldn't do this on my own, and the Bible became my anchor. **Every day, I'd read a verse**, meditate on it, and try to apply it to my life. **Philippians 4:13 (KJV)** became my mantra: *"I can do all things through Christ which strengtheneth me."*

That verse carried me through some of the toughest days. Even though I had been introduced to faith back in 2009, it wasn't until I hit rock bottom in 2021 that I really let it guide me. Faith wasn't just something I talked about anymore—it became the foundation of my recovery, and **Jesus became my strength** when everything else had fallen apart.

Chapter 5

Spiritual Authority – Power in Faith

Once I started leaning into my faith, I realized something that had been missing all along: **spiritual authority**. It wasn't enough to just believe—I had to start walking in the power that God had already given me.

I had spent so much time feeling like a victim of my circumstances—like the bottle had control, the streets had control, even my own thoughts had control over me. But as I grew deeper in my faith, I started to understand that **God had already given me the authority** to take back my life. I just hadn't claimed it yet.

Luke 10:19 (KJV) hit me hard: *"Behold, I give unto you power to tread on serpents and scorpions, and over all the power of the enemy: and nothing shall by any means hurt you."* That wasn't just a metaphor. That was real power—**authority over the things that had been holding me down for years**. God had already handed me the keys, but I wasn't using them. I had spent years **waiting for a way out**, when all along, God had given me the tools to break free.

Stepping into that authority meant I had to **claim it**—I had to take back control of my mind, my actions, and my future. My environment didn't own me. Alcohol didn't own me. The enemy didn't own me. **God's power was bigger than all of it.**

Once I understood that, I started using my faith as more than just a comfort—it became my weapon. **Ephesians 6:16 (KJV)** says, *"Above all, taking the shield of faith, wherewith ye shall be able to quench all the fiery darts of the wicked."* The darts of the wicked weren't always what I thought. Sometimes they were the doubts creeping into my head, telling me I couldn't change. Sometimes they were the temptations to fall back into old habits. **But faith wasn't passive—it was active.**

I had to start speaking with authority over my life. **Proverbs 18:21 (KJV)** says, *"Death and life are in the power of the tongue."* That means what you say matters. If I kept speaking defeat over myself, then that's exactly what I'd get—defeat. But when I started speaking life—when I declared that I was free, that I had power over the things that used to control me—everything started to shift.

Spiritual authority wasn't just about declaring words, though. It was about stepping into the **freedom** God had already promised me. The alcohol, the anxiety, the depression—those were all chains, but they only had power because I kept holding onto them. Once I realized that I had the authority to **break those chains**, everything changed.

I wasn't waiting for God to pull me out of the pit anymore—I realized He had already given me the ladder. All I had to do was climb. **That's what claiming spiritual authority looks like.** It's knowing that God has given you the power to overcome, but it's up to you to use it.

Chapter 6

***

Outgrowing the Streets – Breaking Free from What Held Me

I started to see it before anyone else did—**the streets weren't for me anymore**. For a long time, I had convinced myself that this was my life, that the corner, the drinking, the hanging out, and the way we lived was the only way to be somebody. But deep down, I was starting to feel something different. I began to **despise the street life**—the constant chaos, the cycles of violence, the traps we were falling into.

It was never really about the streets—It was about trying to escape my own reality. **The drinking was a way to numb myself** from the pain I didn't want to face. I had used alcohol to avoid dealing with the **insecurities** and **fears** that I had carried for years. But once I started walking in my faith, once I started connecting with something bigger than myself, I realized I didn't have to keep running.

It wasn't just about faith, though. **The mentors I found along the way**—the ones who showed me there was a different kind of life outside of the streets—became my friends. They were living a different way, showing me what it looked like to walk with purpose and not just survive. They didn't have to tell me to leave the streets behind—they showed me what life could be like on the other side.

That's when I knew I had to get out. The streets weren't a badge of honor anymore—they were a trap, and I couldn't stay in that life any longer. The drinking, the smoking, the endless cycle of trying to numb the pain—it all felt empty. I knew there was something more waiting for me, and the only way I was going to find it was by leaving the environment behind for good.

But it wasn't easy. **My wife and kids didn't understand the changes**. I wasn't the same man I had been when I was hanging out on the corner, and they could see that. **I was changing—becoming a different person**, someone who wasn't content with living in the past or trying to drown my problems in alcohol, even though it still had its grip. I was finally starting to take control of my life, but to them, it felt like I was pulling away.

They didn't understand why I didn't want to hang out with the same people or why I didn't want to be in the same places. They saw this new version of me, and it confused them. But I knew it was necessary. **I couldn't keep living a lie**, pretending like the streets and the bottle were the only way to survive. I had outgrown that life, and I had to start moving in a different direction—whether they understood it or not.

Long story short, **I talked to my wife about leaving the city**. I told her I needed to get out—that we needed a fresh start. To my surprise, she was all in. She didn't push back, didn't question it. We both agreed that we couldn't stay in the same environment anymore. At first, we thought about moving down south, getting a change of scenery somewhere warmer. But instead, we found a house in the mountains of Williamsport.

The mountains felt like the peace we were searching for—a place where I could focus on rebuilding myself and my family. Moving there was the beginning of something new, a step toward living the life I had been seeking all along.

Chapter 7

Wrestling with God – The Power of Prayer

When I began my journey toward sobriety, I realized something early on—**I couldn't do this alone**. I needed a foundation, something solid to hold onto, and that's when I really began to lean into the power of prayer. **It wasn't casual prayer**—it was deep, wrestling with God, seeking real answers, begging for change that would stick. I wasn't just praying for sobriety. I was praying for my family, my marriage, and for God to guide me toward a new life.

One of the first prayers I made was for God to allow me and my wife, **Precious**, to share church together on Sundays. I knew that if we could reconnect through faith, it would be the key to restoring our relationship. But it wasn't going to be easy. Precious had endured a rough childhood, and over the years, that pain turned into **anger and resentment**—especially when it came to the idea of church. I knew it would take a miracle for her to sincerely consider taking this new walk of faith.

And that's exactly what happened—God answered my prayer. At first, Precious didn't realize it, but this was the first **real miracle** I experienced in my recovery. She agreed to start watching **Pastor Mike's sermons** with me every Sunday. It was overwhelming to me because it showed me something so profound: **my wife was willing to follow me**. That realization hit me like a ton of bricks. Up until that point, I had led her through years of chaos, struggle, and pain. But now, through the power of prayer, I was leading her somewhere better. I was leading her to God.

As we watched those sermons together, something began to shift—not just in our relationship, but within myself. **Prayer became my anchor**, the thing that held me together when everything else seemed like it could fall apart. It gave me strength when I felt weak, and it opened up new possibilities where before, I only saw dead ends.

Our marriage started to heal. We found ourselves reconnecting on a spiritual level, sharing conversations about faith, hope, and Praying—things we hadn't previously talked about in our relationship. We was growing. Every Sunday became a time not just to connect with God, but to connect with each other. We weren't just surviving anymore—we were building something new.

But it wasn't just about me and Precious. **I prayed for my kids**, too. I still pray for them every day. They're growing, and I can see God working in their lives, but they're still a work in progress. **I don't want to lose them to this world**, and I'm being real with y'all—that's my greatest fear. I know that all the changes I'm making in my life won't matter if my kids gain the world and lose their souls. So I pray. I ask God to guide them, to protect them, and to help them find their own path to faith, just like He did for me.

Prayer is powerful, and **I'm all in**. If I can lead my family by prayer, then I'm going to keep pushing forward, no matter what comes my way. God showed me that prayer isn't just something we do when we're in trouble—it's how we live every day. It's how we fight for the things that matter most.

Chapter 8

Down the Rabbit Hole – Seeking Truth Beyond the Surface

As I progressed in my recovery, I realized something important—**sobriety was just the beginning**. It wasn't the final destination; it was the starting point of a much deeper journey. Once the fog of addiction began to lift, I found myself yearning for something more. I wasn't just looking for healing—I wanted to understand the world and my place in it in ways I had never explored before.

I started asking God to reveal **deeper truths** to me, and it felt like He opened a floodgate of knowledge. **Jeremiah 33:3 (KJV)** became my compass: *"Call unto me, and I will answer thee, and show thee great and mighty things, which thou knowest not."* It was like doors were opening that I didn't even know existed. Every question I asked seemed to lead to more questions, and every answer felt like a revelation.

One of the first things that hit me was the **danger of living a double-minded life**. The Bible speaks to this in **James 1:8 (KJV):** *"A double-minded man is unstable in all his ways."* I had lived this truth for years—constantly torn between the man I wanted to be and the man I had let myself become. It was like I was living in two worlds, and that instability was holding me back from everything God had for me. But as I dug deeper into God's Word, I felt Him clearing away the clutter in my mind and soul. It was as if He was removing the broken pieces of who I used to be to make room for something better. **Hebrews 10:9 (KJV)** captures it perfectly: *"He taketh away the first, that he may establish the second."*

The more I studied, the more I realized that this journey wasn't just about sobriety—it was about transformation. God wasn't just healing me physically or emotionally; He was **renewing my mind**. He was showing me a new way to think, a new way to live, and a new way to see the world.

I began to dive into things I had never really questioned before. For instance, why did secret societies, like the **Freemasons**, use the King James Bible in their rituals? At first, it didn't make any sense to me. But the more I researched, the more I realized that even the most secretive groups in the world recognize the power of God's Word—even if they twist it for their own purposes. **Job 33:14 (KJV)** says, *"For God speaketh once, yea twice, yet man perceiveth it not."* It reminded me that God's truth is always there, but it's up to us to see it.

I started paying more attention to the **significance of numbers** in the Bible. The number **33** kept popping up—Jesus completed His mission at the age of 33, and the number symbolizes **spiritual enlightenment** and **divine truth**. In **Freemasonry**, the 33rd degree is considered the highest level of enlightenment. It became clear to me that what these secret societies consider hidden or forbidden knowledge is actually **rooted in God's truth**. It wasn't secret at all—it was just waiting for those who were willing to seek it.

But here's what I learned: there was no need to chase after secret knowledge or join exclusive groups to find wisdom. **Proverbs 2:6 (KJV)** says, *"For the LORD giveth wisdom: out of his mouth cometh* *knowledge and understanding.*" God's wisdom isn't hidden behind closed doors or rituals—it's available to everyone who seeks it with a sincere heart. Unlike secret societies, **God invites everyone to receive His wisdom**. There are no barriers or qualifications—just an open heart and a willing spirit.

The more I studied, the more I realized that **this search for knowledge wasn't just about me**. It wasn't about gaining knowledge for knowledge's sake. It was about transformation. **The truth God revealed to me** wasn't meant to be kept hidden or stored away—it was meant to be shared and lived. It wasn't just helping me stay sober; it was giving me the power to reclaim my life and to build a future grounded in faith, hope, and love.

The real strength in knowledge comes from its application. **Proverbs 4:7 (KJV)** says, *"Wisdom is the principal thing; therefore get wisdom: and with all thy getting get understanding."* As I continued to seek, God continued to reveal. And with each revelation, I found more peace, knowing that I was aligned with His will and that everything I needed was already written in His Word.

Chapter 9

Williamsport – A New Beginning Guided by God's Hand

Moving to Williamsport wasn't just a decision—it felt like a divine intervention. After everything my family and I had been through, this move represented a fresh start, a new chapter, and the peace I had been craving for years. **God's hand** was all over it, and I could feel His presence in every step of the process, from finding the house to settling into our new life.

Precious had been saving up for this house, and I'll always be indebted to her for that. She believed in this move just as much as I did, and her support was everything. It was as if God was giving me peace through my wife, showing me that I wasn't in this journey alone. We had come a long way from the chaos of the streets and the struggles of the city, and now we were finally stepping into something better—together.

Williamsport had its own issues, of course. Like any place, there were challenges. **Some areas had a drug problem**, and it wasn't like we were completely leaving behind the struggles of the world. But the neighborhood we found was **quiet, peaceful**, and exactly what we needed. It wasn't about escaping reality—it was about creating a new one, a healthier, more stable environment for my family.

Before moving to Williamsport, I had been working as a **private contractor**, and that work had been a blessing financially. But it wasn't helping with my **social isolation**. I spent most of my time working alone, which kept me distant from people, even though I was making good money. When we moved, I made a conscious decision to try working around other people. **It wasn't about the money anymore**—it was about the quality of life. I wanted to stay close to home, and I knew it would do me some good to connect with others again.

Things started going well. It was like God had locked me into position, setting me up for something greater. I was helping to build something, contributing to the growth of the company, and for the first time in a long time, I felt **appreciated**. It wasn't just a job—it was a place where I could grow, both professionally and personally. **God was moving** in my life, and one of the clearest signs of that was my supervisor—a woman of faith, fair and just. I seen Gods hand painting a new picture in my life, In real time. I wasn't just working a job—I was finding family.

Then came the article. I made the front page of the company's article, and at first, it didn't seem like a big deal. I brushed it off, thinking it was just a small thing. But as time passed, I realized it was more than that—it was a reminder of how far I'd come. Through faith I tore down a stronghold in my life. God had taken me from a place of isolation and depression, and now I was being recognized—not for the mistakes of my past, but for the **progress of my present**.

I also learned to **embrace the good things** happening in my life, the same way I had spent years focusing on the bad. It was a sense of **duality**—life wasn't just about the struggles and the hard times; it was about victories, blessings, and growth. I had to make a choice: keep focusing on what caused my depression, or start celebrating the good. **I chose the latter**.

But God didn't stop there. In addition to my job, I started my own online business. It had been something I prayed for back in 2008—long before I even thought sobriety was possible. I had always been fascinated with computers, and I had a knack for marketing, but nothing ever really took off. But now, in this new season of my life, it all started to come together. **I invested in my own product**, and a few months later, I sold nearly 1,000 units. You might have heard of the brand **Shiddy Shawp**—yeah, that's me.

It was amazing to see the work I had put in finally pay off, but it wasn't just about the money or the success—it was about seeing God's faithfulness, the designers hand in action. He had heard my prayers years ago, even when I wasn't ready to receive the blessings. Now, after all this time, He was delivering on His promises.

And now, here I am, writing this book. **This book wouldn't exist without God**. Every page, every chapter, is a testimony to His power and His grace. It's a testament to what can happen when you step out in faith, when you follow His guidance, and when you trust that He has a plan for your life—even when it feels like everything is falling apart.

Moving to Williamsport wasn't just about finding a new place to live. **It was about finding peace**—peace with myself, peace with my family, and peace with God. It was about creating a new foundation, one built on faith, healing, and a renewed sense of purpose. God guided us here, and because of that, I know that this is just the beginning of what He has in store.

Chapter 10

The Strength of Vulnerability

As I began to heal and grow, one truth kept hitting me harder than I expected—**vulnerability is not a weakness**. In fact, it turned out to be one of the most powerful tools I had in my arsenal. For most of my life, I thought being strong meant keeping everything bottled up, putting on a tough face, and handling things on my own. I thought that's what made you a man. But looking back, that toughness wasn't real—it was just a mask, hiding the pain, fear, and confusion I didn't want to deal with.

When I finally allowed myself to be vulnerable, to open up about my struggles, my fears, and the battles going on inside my head, it was like a weight had been lifted. **The relief was almost instant**. The people I opened up to responded with support instead of judgment. They encouraged me, prayed for me, and suddenly, I realized—I didn't have to carry this burden alone. **Proverbs 28:13 (KJV)** says, *"He that covereth his sins shall not prosper: but whoso confesseth and forsaketh them shall have mercy."* It was true. **Being real about my weaknesses** brought me closer to God, and it brought me closer to the people who really cared.

Before, I was terrified of being vulnerable. I thought if I showed weakness, people would see me as less of a man. But it was the opposite—**vulnerability became my strength**. When I let go of the pride and the front, I found real connections with people who were struggling just like I was. And it wasn't about being perfect. It was about being real, letting people know that it's okay to admit you're not okay. **That's where the real strength lies**—not in pretending you've got it all together, but in finding the courage to say you need help.

2 Corinthians 12:9 (KJV) hit home for me: *"And he said unto me, My grace is sufficient for thee: for my strength is made perfect in weakness."* The moment I realized that **my strength came from acknowledging my weakness**, everything changed. It wasn't about proving myself to anyone anymore—it was about letting God's grace work through my brokenness.

When I started sharing my story, people didn't look down on me like I thought they would. They responded with compassion. They opened up to me in return, and we began to build **real, authentic relationships**. It was the kind of connection I hadn't felt in years. That sense of community, of knowing I wasn't alone, was life-changing. I started to see that by showing others my true self, I wasn't exposing weakness—I was letting **God's grace shine through**.

Vulnerability wasn't a road to shame—it was a road to healing. The more I opened up, the more I realized that others were walking the same path, fighting the same fight. Together, we could lean on each other, pray for each other, and keep each other going. It wasn't about trying to survive in isolation anymore—it was about surviving as part of a community, knowing that we were all in this together.

James 5:16 (KJV) tells us to *"Confess your faults one to another, and pray one for another, that ye may be healed."* Healing came through vulnerability—through opening up and trusting that God could use my brokenness for His glory. And that's exactly what He did. The more I let go of my need to control everything, the more God stepped in and gave me the strength to keep going.

One of the greatest lessons I learned was that **vulnerability doesn't mean giving up control**. It means trusting God enough to let go of the mask and allow His strength to carry me. And when I did that, I wasn't walking this journey alone. I realized that others were fighting the same battles, and together, we could support each other in ways that made the journey easier to bear.

When I opened up to **Precious**, that was a major turning point. I had spent so long trying to shield her from the depth of my struggles, thinking I was protecting her. But in reality, I was shutting her out. When I finally let her in, we connected on a deeper level than ever before. She saw the real me—the man who was hurting, but trying to heal. The man who was fighting his demons, but still standing. That vulnerability brought us closer, and it showed me that being real with her was the key to strengthening our relationship.

Being vulnerable—with God, with Precious, with the people around me—was one of the most powerful decisions I ever made. It wasn't easy, and it wasn't something that came naturally. But once I embraced it, everything changed. The strength I found in my weakness, the connections I built through being real, and the healing I experienced by trusting God with my brokenness—**that's where true transformation began.**

Chapter 11

✦

Fighting the Hurt – Trigger Warning

When I talk about **fighting the hurt**, I'm talking about the relentless battle that happens inside your head. It's that overwhelming mix of emotions—the "What Ifs," the "Why Mes," and the constant second-guessing of yourself. Addiction doesn't come alone. It drags **depression and anxiety** into the ring, turning your mind into a battlefield. And it doesn't matter what kind of addiction you're dealing with—whether it's alcohol, drugs, or something else. With addiction comes the mental war, and it's designed to take you out.

Depression makes you feel like you're stuck in a bottomless pit—like there's nothing good left to happen. You start believing that life is over before it's even really begun. On the flip side, **anxiety** has you convinced that bad things are definitely coming. You feel it in your bones, like disaster is lurking around the corner. That constant tension becomes your new normal, and you start manifesting your worst fears. The mind is powerful, and when it gets twisted by addiction and pain, it creates the very things you're afraid of.

We'll get into more about how that works later, but trust me—your mind creates realities you don't even realize.

The cycle is **vicious**. You start questioning your sanity. "What's wrong with me? Why do I feel like I'm losing control?" Addiction pulls you deeper into that rabbit hole. You compare yourself to others: "Look at him, smiling like life is good. Look at what he's doing for his family. Why am I not there?"

I remember those days vividly. I'd sit there, thinking, **I'm holding my wife back. I'm too far gone. I'll never catch up to the life I should've had**. These thoughts came like clockwork—especially when I was trying to function without alcohol in my system. It's a loop that keeps spinning in your mind, convincing you that there's no way out.

Let me pause here and be clear—**these weren't casual thoughts**. These were thoughts that consumed me. They pushed me to the brink of what felt like insanity. There were days when I didn't know if I'd ever come back. People on the outside probably thought I'd lost it completely.

But I wasn't done fighting. **Fighting the hurt** became my motto, my battle cry. It wasn't just about the addiction anymore. It was about pushing back against the pain and the doubts that tried to corner me. **Why are they so happy? Why am I not?** That hurt, that isolation, it whispered in my ear: **I'm going to ruin your life, and no one can help you**. And here's the thing—I wasn't alone in feeling like that. Not by a long shot.

Depression, anxiety, and addiction all have one thing in common—they isolate you. They make you feel like you're the only one going through it. But when I started opening up, when I started talking about what I was feeling, I realized that other people had been walking through the same storm. **I wasn't the only one** dealing with these struggles, and that realization gave me the strength to keep fighting.

Breaking Free from the Hurt

Here's the truth—**fighting the hurt is temporary**, but the battle is for your life. Depression and anxiety, like addiction, are often the last line of defense before you break through. Once you push past that overwhelming pain, once you stop hiding from it and start facing it head-on, things start to change. **The clouds lift**, the fog begins to clear, and you start to see who you really are without the chains of addiction weighing you down.

It's like reaching through the flames to save something valuable—something you can't afford to lose. And that something is **your life**. You're pulling yourself back from the edge, back from the destruction that addiction, depression, and anxiety have tried to lead you toward.

My Journey—A Bachelor's Degree in Survival

Let me be real with y'all—my story of recovery isn't just about quitting alcohol. It's about **surviving the mental battles** that came with it. My experiences feel like I earned a degree in survival psychology, except I didn't get it from any school or program. I got it from walking through the fire, from battling my way through addiction and depression. **My scars are my credentials**, and they allow me to speak truth to those who are still out there fighting their own battles.

This fight gave me something priceless—the ability to say, **I've been through it, and I made it out**. That's the gift God gave me, and I'm using it to show others that recovery is not only possible—it's necessary. Just as I was saved, I want to be a light for others, showing them that they can push past the pain and reclaim their lives.

Chapter 12

—✦—

Building on Success

S uccess isn't a final destination—it's a series of steps, of small victories that build on each other. In recovery, every win, no matter how small, is a brick in the foundation of something bigger. And here's what I've learned—**you can't get stuck celebrating too long**, but you also can't ignore the wins you've fought for. **Philippians 3:13-14 (KJV)** became my guide: *"Brethren, I count not myself to have apprehended: but this one thing I do, forgetting those things which are behind, and reaching forth unto those things which are before, I press toward the mark for the prize of the high calling of God in Christ Jesus."*

That's how I saw my journey. I was pressing forward, brick by brick, building a new life. And every day that I chose sobriety, every day that I chose faith over fear, I was adding to that foundation. **Success isn't a straight line**. There were times I stumbled, times I relapsed. But every time I got back up, I learned something new, and I kept building.

When the pandemic hit in 2020, it felt like life was **thrown into chaos**. My job shut down, and like everyone else, I had to figure things out. That's when I started driving for **Lyft**. My wife was out there working in one of the hardest-hit areas, **Kensington**, one of

Philly's roughest neighborhoods. It was a place filled with crime, drugs, and violence. I spent a lot of time driving through those streets, and it was there, in that environment, that I began opening up about my own battles with alcohol.

I started talking to the people who rode with me. People who were just trying to survive, like I was. I'd tell them about my fight with addiction, about the idea of the **inner man versus the outer man**, and how I was learning to align those two through faith. And the wild thing? **People responded**. I'd have riders in my car telling me, "Man, I needed to hear that," or, "It feels like God sent you today."

It hit me that my story wasn't just for me. **God was using my testimony to touch others**. Some of the toughest people, the ones the world had labeled as "lost causes," would open up to me. They'd tell me things I didn't expect to hear. It reminded me that God's Word is powerful, even when we don't see the immediate results.

But as much as I was witnessing to others, I wasn't fully out of the storm myself. **I relapsed at the end of 2020**, right around Christmas and New Year's. I thought I could handle just one drink, but it spiraled fast. That temporary success I'd built seemed to slip right through my hands, and I fell back into the same pit I'd been climbing out of.

I felt the **weight of failure**. That familiar shame crept in, and I went back to my old habits for a while. It wasn't until January 12, 2021, that I finally quit drinking for good. This time, I knew I couldn't half-step it. I had to fully surrender—**I had to let God take the wheel**. There was no more room for trying to do it on my own.

By then, the pandemic had isolated me even further. My work with **Lyft** slowed down, and the people I had been witnessing to were no longer there. I started feeling that familiar anxiety creep back in—**the isolation, the doubt**. But something was different this time. I had the tools now. I had **faith** and a deeper understanding of who I was. I wasn't the same person I'd been when I first started this journey.

That's when I decided to **start a YouTube channel**. I called it **Quit Drinking With Bible**, and it was my way of continuing the conversation I had been having with people in my car. Facing the camera for the first time was like looking into a mirror—a mirror I hadn't wanted to look into for years. Seeing my own face reminded me of all the damage alcohol had done. But I knew I had to push through that discomfort. I had to tell my story, not just for me, but for the people who needed to hear it.

To my surprise, the feedback started pouring in. People were **thanking me** for sharing my story, telling me how much it helped them. One person even wrote, *"You give hope to people with your same struggle... continue spreading your message, God has a plan for you."*

That's when it hit me—**my success wasn't just about quitting alcohol**. It was about using my experiences to help others overcome their own struggles. Every step I took in my recovery, every day I chose sobriety, wasn't just a win for me. It was a win for everyone who heard my story and found hope in it.

Success isn't just about reaching the top. It's about **building something lasting**. Every small victory in sobriety, every conversation on YouTube, every connection with someone who's fighting their own battle—it's all part of something bigger. And I'm not just building for myself. **I'm building for my family**, for my community, and for anyone who comes after me. Each success, each milestone, is a testament to God's grace and His work in my life.

Chapter 13

Passing It On

As I've walked this road of recovery, one thing has become clear—**my story isn't just mine**. The life I've lived, the struggles I've faced, and the victories I've won—they all have a purpose beyond me. I'm a walking testimony for everyone who's watched me fall and rise again. I've become living proof that **transformation is possible**.

If even **one person** sees the change in me and feels inspired, then I've done my job. That one spark of hope can ignite a fire in someone else's life. And that fire can spread—to their children, their grandchildren, and beyond. **That's legacy**. It's passing down more than just a story; it's passing down hope. **Hope is contagious**, and when you pass it on, it multiplies.

Jeremiah 1:5 (KJV) says, *"Before I formed thee in the belly I knew thee."* God has a plan for all of us, even when we're too lost in the struggle to see it. And when you make it through your darkest days, you owe it to the people who are still stuck in theirs to pass on what you've learned. **1 Corinthians 10:13 (KJV)** promises, *"God is faithful, who will not suffer you to be tempted above that ye are* *able.*" That's real. The battles we face are never more than we can handle—with God on our side, **nothing is impossible**.

I look back at the old me, the guy who thought the streets were everything, who couldn't see beyond the bottle, and I realize something—**I was fighting God**. I was fighting the idea that something bigger than me was in control. The moment I stopped resisting, the moment I let God take over, everything started to change. It's like I had been swimming upstream, exhausted and barely staying afloat. But when I finally surrendered to God, it was like the current flipped in my favor. The struggle wasn't gone, but I wasn't fighting it alone anymore.

Passing it on isn't just about telling people how to recover. It's about showing them that their lives have meaning—that no matter how far they've fallen, they can rise again. My YouTube channel, **Quit Drinking With Bible**, is just one way I've been able to pass on what I've learned. Every video, every comment, every conversation is a chance to **plant a seed**. It's not up to me to make that seed grow—that's between them and God—but I'm here to plant it. And I trust that God will handle the rest.

When I think about the people I've connected with, the ones who've reached out to me saying, **"Your story saved me"**, I realize how important it is to keep sharing. This isn't just about me—it's about everyone who's still in the trenches, fighting their way out. I know what that fight feels like, and I'm here to show them that it's worth it.

But it's not just about addiction. This journey, this legacy of hope, extends beyond alcohol or drugs. It's about fighting for your life, your purpose, your future. It's about breaking free from anything that's holding you back, whether it's depression, anxiety, trauma, or a toxic environment. **We are all called to something greater**, and part of my calling is to help others see that in themselves.

James 2:17 (KJV) says, *"Even so faith, if it hath not works, is dead, being alone."* My faith isn't just something I talk about—it's something I live out every day. And part of that faith is **doing the work**, passing on the knowledge, the hope, and the grace that God has given me.

Passing it on is about leaving a trail of light behind you, so others can follow. It's about being the person you needed when you were lost. It's about **becoming the proof** that change is possible, no matter how dark it gets. That's the mission I'm on. And I'll keep sharing my story until everyone who needs to hear it has heard it.

Chapter 14

The Importance of Faith

If there's one thing that's been a constant throughout my journey, it's **faith**. Faith wasn't just something I learned about in church—it became the foundation of everything I've achieved, from overcoming addiction to rebuilding my life and my family. **Faith** is the fuel that carried me through the darkest moments, gave me the strength to keep going, and allowed me to see a future where sobriety was possible.

But here's the thing—**faith isn't just about belief**. It's about **trusting God** with every part of your life, even the messy parts. It's easy to trust God when things are going well, but when you're deep in the struggle, when you can't see a way out, that's when faith becomes real. **Hebrews 11:1 (KJV)** says, *"Now faith is the substance of things hoped for, the evidence of things not seen."* Faith is believing that there's a way out, even when you can't see it yet.

For me, faith was the only thing that kept me moving forward. When I didn't have the answers, when I couldn't see a clear path, I had to trust that **God was making a way**. That's what faith looks like in real life—it's walking forward in hope, not because you see the end, but because you trust that God will get you there.

Philippians 4:13 (KJV) became my life verse: *"I can do all things through Christ which strengtheneth me."* That's what kept me going.

Faith wasn't just about **staying sober**—it was about **transforming** every part of my life. There's a difference between just quitting alcohol and actually letting God take over. Quitting alcohol was the first step, but faith is what allowed me to rebuild everything I had lost. It gave me the strength to become the man God had called me to be. Faith gave me a vision for my future when I couldn't see one for myself.

When I think back to my days in the streets, faith wasn't really on my radar. I was too busy running from it. But even in those moments, **God was still there**, keeping me from falling all the way off the edge. The prayers my grandmother prayed for me, the times when things could've gone way worse but didn't—that was God at work, even when I wasn't paying attention.

Faith is what carries you through when everything else falls apart. It's what gives you the strength to keep fighting when your body and mind are tired. And when you lean into it, when you trust God with everything, **it transforms you**. It's not about being perfect—it's about being willing to let God step into your mess and turn it into something better.

For me, faith wasn't just a **safety net**; it was a weapon. It was what I used to fight off the old temptations, the old habits. Every time the bottle tried to call me back, I had to remind myself that I wasn't doing this alone. **God had my back**, and because of that, I could walk away from the things that had once kept me trapped.

Faith in Action

But faith isn't just something you feel—it's something you **live out**. It's a daily choice to trust God, even when you don't have all the answers. It's getting up every morning and deciding that no matter what, you're going to follow God's plan for your life. And sometimes that's hard, especially when things aren't going the way you expected.

But here's the thing—**faith doesn't fail**. Even when we fall, even when we mess up, **God's still there**. He never gives up on us, even when we're ready to give up on ourselves. And that's why faith is so important. It's the foundation we build everything else on.

Proverbs 3:5-6 (KJV) reminds us, *"Trust in the LORD with all thine heart; and lean not unto thine own understanding. In all thy ways acknowledge him, and he shall direct thy paths."* Faith isn't about figuring it all out on your own—it's about trusting that **God's got a plan**, and He's guiding you every step of the way.

And trust me, when you live with that kind of faith, you'll see God move in ways you never expected. I've seen it in my life, and I know it's real.

Chapter 15

✦

Staying the Course

We've come a long way, and I'll be the first to tell you—**staying the course is no joke**. Recovery isn't a straight line. It's a road filled with twists, turns, and setbacks. But one thing I've learned is this: **you have to keep pushing**. It doesn't matter how many times you fall; it matters how many times you get back up. Every time you get up, you're staying the course.

And here's the thing—**old habits don't die easily**. The years of addiction, the bad decisions, the negative thinking—they don't just disappear overnight. You have to constantly renew your mind, body, and spirit. The Bible teaches us that **renewing the mind** is key to real change. As long as we occupy this earthly body, there's always room to grow, learn, and recover. **Romans 12:2 (KJV)** reminds us, *"And be not conformed to this world: but be ye transformed by the renewing of your mind, that ye may prove what is that good, and acceptable, and perfect, will of God."* That transformation doesn't happen once—it's ongoing.

Every day is an opportunity to engage in positive actions. Whether it's through prayer, reading the Word, or surrounding yourself with people who lift you up, you have to stay connected to your faith. That's how you stay the course.

Recovery isn't a destination—it's a journey. And it's one I'm committed to for the rest of my life. Sure, there are still days when I struggle with the flashbacks of anxiety, depression, and when the old temptations try to sneak back in. But I've learned that the key to staying on track is to stay grounded in my faith. I have to keep my eyes on Jesus and surround myself with people who encourage me to keep going forward not backwards, even on the toughest days.

The Bible says in **Hebrews 12:1 (KJV)**, *"Wherefore seeing we also are compassed about with so great a cloud of witnesses, let us lay aside every weight, and the sin which doth so easily beset us, and let us run with patience the race that is set before us."* This journey is a race, and I'm running it with patience, knowing that each step moves me closer to the life God has called me to live.

As I continue to walk this path, I'm always reminded of one thing: **your story matters**. Your experiences—the ups, the downs, the wins, the losses—they are all a part of what makes you who you are. And those experiences? They have value. Someone out there needs to hear them, just like I needed to hear the stories of others who walked this road before me.

Your testimony is a gift, and it's meant to be shared. The more you share it, the more you help others see that they're not alone. **You become the evidence** that no matter how hard life gets, it's possible to come out on the other side stronger and better.

Faith isn't a one-time event. It's something you choose daily. You have to wake up every morning and make the decision to keep fighting, to stay sober, to trust in God's plan. It's not easy, but it's worth it.

Chapter 16

Be Careful What You Follow

This ain't a novel, y'all. This is my story. And just like my story, the trauma hit quick and swift. Twenty-five years of my life— gone in the blink of an eye. Relationships with family and friends? Gone. My kids' school years? Missed. And all because I let time slip away while I was caught up in the wrong things.

I say this to remind you—**time moves fast**. Before you know it, it's gone. I'm almost 50 now, and I see history repeating itself over and over again. The trends may have changed—maybe it's not 40 ounces anymore, maybe it's all about "Turning Up," partying, and whatever else the culture's pushing. But here's the truth: **you need to be careful what you follow**.

You are the **creator of your own reality**. The decisions you make today are shaping your tomorrow. And if you don't like what's happening in your life right now, guess what? Just like changing the channel on a TV, you can **change your life** with one decision. Every choice you make is steering you toward a future that either empowers you or keeps you stuck. The power is in your hands.

Jesus himself said, *"Is it not written in your law, I said, Ye are gods?"* (John 10:34 KJV). You were made in the image of an Almighty God:

"So God created man in his own image, in the image of God created he him; male and female created he them" (Genesis 1:27 KJV). And nothing you imagine will be withheld from you: *"And the LORD said, Behold, the people is one, and they have all one language; and this they begin to do: and now nothing will be restrained from them, which they have imagined to do"* (Genesis 11:6 KJV). That's the power you hold—what you think, you manifest.

If you want to get high, if you want to party and get drunk—guess what? **It will not be withheld from you**. The world, through music, TV, and trends, will be right there to advertise these things to you. They know how easily you'll follow. Most of the time, it's all about money, but sometimes it's about control. The people running this world have more confidence in your power to create than you do. They know once they plant the seed of a suggestion, you'll take it and finish the story on your own. But you've got the power to **change the narrative**.

Control your reality. Just like you can imagine yourself walking into a bar or heading to your dealer's house, you can project yourself toward your goals. The tricky part is, if you focus on how hard it's going to be, then "hard" is exactly what you'll get. Don't fall for the same tricks I did. **Satan is slick**. He doesn't change God's Word—he twists it. **Genesis 3:1 (KJV)** says, *"Now the serpent was more subtil than any beast of the field which the LORD God had made. And he said unto the woman, Yea, hath God said, Ye shall not eat of every tree of the garden?"* Don't let him twist your reality.

Take back your power. Rule over your life, and if you fall, get back up. Get better or die trying. You're worth it. Your life is worth it. Don't let anyone or anything tell you otherwise.

This was JuiceDaMac, y'all. Shout out to TRE0-OX, where it all started. Moment of silence for the many lost but never forgotten. I love y'all. **Peace, and I'm out.**

Section 2

THE INNER MAN VS. THE OUTER MAN

Now that y'all know my story, I'm going to leave y'all with some empowering things to think about. We're about to go deep—**real deep**. What's next is more than just the struggles, the highs, and the lows I've already shared. **In this section, we're diving into the real battle that each of us faces daily—the battle between the inner man and the outer man.**

It's about the struggle that goes beyond addiction, beyond the streets, beyond the surface. **This battle is spiritual, and it's the fight for your very soul.** We're going to talk about how to strengthen the inner man and overcome the things that have been controlling your life. **We're going deep, and we're going to expose the truth of what's been holding you back—and more importantly, how you can break free.**

Chapter 1

✦

The Battle Between Flesh and Spirit

Alright, so now that we've laid the groundwork, it's time to talk about something real. **I'm talking about the battle that's always raging inside us—the battle between the inner man and the outer man.**

This battle isn't just about the obvious things like addiction or temptation. It's deeper than that. It's about the constant war between who you really are deep down inside—the person God created you to be—and the version of you that the world tries to mold. **It's the fight between your spirit and your flesh.**

The Outer Man: The Flesh Wants Control

First, let's talk about the outer man—the flesh. This is the side of you that's always chasing after what feels good in the moment. The flesh is that part of you that craves instant gratification, whether it's the bottle, the money, the status, or anything else that promises a quick fix.

Trust me, I know all about it. For years, I was chasing whatever I thought would numb the pain or make me feel like I had it all together. But here's the thing—no matter how much I fed the flesh, it was never enough. It's like pouring water into a cup with a hole in it. You can keep filling it up, but it'll never stay full.

Romans 7:18 (KJV) says, "For I know that in me (that is, in my flesh,) dwelleth no good thing: for to will is present with me; but how to perform that which is good I find not."

Paul was breaking it down right there—the flesh doesn't have anything good to offer. **It might promise you everything, but it'll leave you with nothing.** The more you give into it, the more control it takes. That's what was happening to me. The more I let my outer man run things, the more I lost sight of who I really was.

The Inner Man: Your Spirit Wants to Be Free

Now, let's flip it. The inner man—your spirit—is the part of you that's connected to God. This is the real you, the you that was created for something greater. The problem is, we live in a world that's always feeding the outer man and starving the inner man. We get so caught up in what we can see, touch, and feel that we forget there's a whole other part of us that's trying to break free.

Ephesians 3:16 (KJV) says, "That he would grant you, according to the riches of his glory, to be strengthened with might by his Spirit in the inner man."

That right there is the key—your inner man has to be strengthened. **And the only way to do that is through God's Spirit.** Your spirit is where your faith lives, where your purpose is found. But if your outer man is running the show, your inner man never gets a chance to rise up and take its rightful place.

The War Within

Here's the truth: every day, there's a war going on inside you. The outer man wants control, and it'll do whatever it takes to keep you focused on what's right in front of you—your problems, your cravings, your past. **But the inner man is fighting to break free, to remind you that you're more than what you've been through.**

It's easy to get caught up in what the outer man wants. I've been there. But I'm here to tell you, the real power comes from feeding the inner man. **The more you strengthen your spirit, the less control the flesh has over you.** The battle is real, but so is the victory.

How This Connects to Recovery

When I was struggling with addiction, I was living in the flesh. **My outer man was running the show**, making me chase things that were killing me. But as I started to grow in my faith, I realized something—the more I fed my inner man, the less power my outer man had over me. It didn't happen overnight, but little by little, my spirit began to take control.

Recovery isn't just about stopping the behavior. **It's about understanding that there's a battle going on inside you,** and the only way to win is by strengthening your inner man. It's about waking up every day and choosing to feed your spirit, not your flesh.

What You Can Do Right Now

So how do you feed your inner man? How do you start winning the war within? Here's what worked for me:

- **Get Into the Word:** The Bible is food for your inner man. The more you read, the more you're giving your spirit the strength it needs to fight back. Start small if you have to, but get into it. Matthew 4:4 (KJV) says, "Man shall not live by bread alone, but by every word that proceedeth out of the mouth of God."
- **Pray for Strength:** You can't do this on your own. Ask God to strengthen your inner man. Ask Him to give you the power to overcome the flesh and live in the spirit.
- **Stay Focused on What Matters:** The outer man wants to distract you with temporary things. But you've got to keep your eyes on the bigger picture. **You're not just fighting to stay clean—you're fighting to become the person God created you to be.**

Takeaway: The Battle Is Yours to Win

The battle between your inner man and outer man is real, but so is your power to win. **The more you feed your spirit, the stronger you'll get.** And as your inner man grows, the outer man will lose its grip on your life.

This is your fight. But it's a fight you can win.

Chapter 2

The Battle of the Mind

Now that we've laid down the foundation of the inner man and the outer man, it's time to go deeper. See, the real struggle between these two isn't just happening in the choices we make, the habits we're trying to break, or the temptations we're fighting. The real battlefield? It's your mind.

Your thoughts are where everything starts. It's where your inner man and outer man wage war day in and day out. What you think, what you allow to take up space in your mind—that's where the power struggle between the flesh and the spirit truly happens.

The Mind is Where the War is Won or Lost

Here's the thing: the streets, the people you hang with, even the situations you find yourself in—those are just the results of what's already happening in your mind. The outer man is loud, always trying to get your attention, always dragging you toward what feels good in the moment. That's the flesh. It's always calling for a quick fix—a way to numb the pain, to find comfort, to run from reality.

But the inner man? That's the part of you that wants more. That's the part of you that knows there's a higher calling, that you were made for something greater. And while the outer man thrives on what's easy and what's temporary, the inner man is built for endurance, for strength, and for purpose.

In Romans 8:5 (KJV), it says, *"For they that are after the flesh do mind the things of the flesh; but they that are after the Spirit the things of the Spirit."* That right there is the blueprint for the war in your mind. If your mind is constantly locked in on what the flesh wants, that's all you'll chase. But if you start feeding your spirit, renewing your mind, that's where the real transformation happens.

Renewing Your Mind: Breaking the Cycle

This is where renewing your mind comes in. It's not just about fighting the same battle over and over—it's about changing the way you think. The Bible tells us in Romans 12:2 (KJV), *"And be not conformed to this world: but be ye transformed by the renewing of your mind."*

To break free from the grip of the outer man, you've got to renew your mind daily. It's about taking control of your thoughts, refusing to let the flesh have the final say. Your thoughts feed your spirit, or they feed your flesh—there's no in-between. If your mind is always focused on what the world offers, the outer man will always win. But if you set your mind on what God's got for you, the inner man will rise up, and that's where your true strength comes from.

The Power of Thoughts

Everything starts with a thought. Before you even act, before you speak, it begins in your mind. What you entertain up there is what will eventually manifest in your actions and your life. That's why this battle is so critical. It's not just about avoiding bad decisions or staying out of trouble—it's about winning the war before it even begins.

In 2 Corinthians 10:5 (KJV), it says, *"Casting down imaginations, and every high thing that exalteth itself against the knowledge of God, and bringing into captivity every thought to the obedience of Christ."* Every thought that comes through your mind needs to be checked, because if you let the wrong ones grow unchecked, they become strongholds.

Strongholds are more than just bad habits or negative emotions—they're mental prisons. The outer man loves strongholds because they keep you stuck. They make you believe that the situation you're in is permanent, that you can't change, that the addictions, the failures, and the pain will always define you. But that's a lie, and it's one the outer man uses to keep you in chains.

Reprogramming Your Mind for Victory

Breaking those strongholds starts with reprogramming your mind. It's about feeding the inner man with the right thoughts and starving the outer man by refusing to entertain the lies.

Here's how it works: Every day, you've got to make a choice. You can either give your thoughts over to the things of the flesh—fear, doubt, anger, lust—or you can focus on the things of the spirit—faith, hope, love, and purpose. This is how you break the cycle, by deciding what gets to live in your mind.

The Bible says in Philippians 4:8 (KJV), *"Whatsoever things are true, whatsoever things are honest, whatsoever things are just, whatsoever things are pure, whatsoever things are lovely, whatsoever things are of good report; if there be any virtue, and if there be any praise, think on these things."* This is your roadmap for reprogramming your mind. What you focus on will grow. If you keep your mind fixed on things that build you up, that strengthen your spirit, the inner man will grow stronger, and the outer man will lose its grip on your life.

How This Plays Out in Your Life

Think about it—when you're stuck in addiction or locked in negative cycles, where's your mind at? Nine times out of ten, it's focused on what's right in front of you—the pain, the temptation, the struggle. You get stuck replaying the same thoughts, the same memories, the same failures. The outer man feeds off this, dragging you deeper into the cycle.

But what happens when you shift your focus? When you start filling your mind with thoughts of where you're going instead of where you've been? When you begin to believe that you're more than your mistakes? That's when the change starts. The outer man loses its power because you're no longer giving it control over your mind.

This is what happened in my life. For years, I was trapped by the thoughts of the flesh, always focused on what I couldn't change, on the pain I was carrying, on the mistakes I had made. But when I started renewing my mind, when I started choosing to think about my future, about the life God had for me, that's when things began to shift. I stopped living for the moment and started living for the purpose.

The Practical Side of Winning the Battle

Let's keep it real—this isn't an overnight thing. Renewing your mind is a daily choice. The outer man isn't just going to disappear because you've had a few good days. You've got to stay consistent, stay vigilant, and stay committed to feeding the inner man. So how do you do that practically?

Here are a few things that worked for me:

1. **Surround Yourself with the Right Voices**: The people you let into your life have a huge impact on your thoughts. Are they feeding your spirit, or are they feeding your flesh? Are they lifting you up, or dragging you down? You've got to be intentional about who you let speak into your life.

2. **Get Into the Word**: The Bible is your weapon in this battle. The more you fill your mind with scripture, the more you arm the inner man for victory. It's not just about memorizing verses—it's about letting God's truth reshape the way you think.

3. **Take Your Thoughts Captive**: Every time a thought comes in that doesn't line up with God's truth, you've got to capture it. Don't let it run wild. Don't let it build a stronghold. Speak truth over that lie, and replace it with what God says about you.

4. **Pray Without Ceasing**: Prayer is more than just talking to God—it's keeping your mind focused on Him throughout the day. When you stay connected to God in prayer, the outer man has less room to operate.

Takeaway: Your Mind is the Key to Freedom

At the end of the day, the battle between the inner man and the outer man is all about what's going on in your mind. Win the battle in your thoughts, and you'll win the battle in your life. The outer man will always try to take control, but the inner man has the strength to overcome, as long as you keep feeding it the right things.

So ask yourself: What's feeding your mind today? Are you letting the outer man win by focusing on what the flesh wants, or are you renewing your mind and letting the inner man take its rightful place? The choice is yours, and it's one you've got to make every single day.

Chapter 3

The Masks We Wear

We've been talking about the war between the inner man and the outer man—the battle between your spirit and your flesh. But here's another layer to this battle that we don't often recognize, and it's just as dangerous: the masks we wear.

For a long time, I was wearing a mask, hiding my true self from the world and even from myself. On the outside, it looked like I had it all together. I had a legit hustle, my street credibility, and I projected confidence, but deep down? I was struggling. I was lost. The image I projected to the world was just a mask—a way to cover up the pain, the fear, and the uncertainty that was eating me alive.

Why We Wear Masks

We all wear masks for different reasons. Some of us are afraid that people won't accept us for who we really are. Some of us are scared to be vulnerable because it feels like if we show our real selves, we'll get hurt. And some of us wear masks because we're trying to live up to an image that the world has pushed on us.

For me, the mask I wore was built from years of trying to survive in the streets. I thought that if I looked strong, if I acted like nothing could touch me, I'd be safe. But inside, I was dealing with self-doubt, fear, and the weight of not knowing what my real purpose was. I was hiding my struggles because I didn't want anyone to see the cracks in my armor.

The Bible talks about this in Ephesians 4:22-24 (KJV): "That ye put off concerning the former conversation the old man, which is corrupt according to the deceitful lusts; And be renewed in the spirit of your mind; And that ye put on the new man, which after God is created in righteousness and true holiness."

It's telling us to take off the mask, the version of ourselves that's been corrupted by the world. The new man, the real you, is who God created you to be—full of righteousness and holiness. It's time to stop hiding and start walking in that truth.

The False Identity of the Outer Man

Here's the truth: the outer man loves the mask. It's all about appearances—about looking like you've got it together, even when you're falling apart inside. The outer man is concerned with what people think, how people see you, and it wants you to believe that your value is in what you have, what you've accomplished, or how strong you appear to others.

But that's a false identity. It's not who you really are. The outer man is the version of you that the world created, and as long as you keep living in that identity, you'll never be free.

2 Corinthians 5:17 (KJV) says, "Therefore if any man be in Christ, he is a new creature: old things are passed away; behold, all things are become new." That's the truth about your identity. The old, false version of you? It's gone. The real you is the new creature, created by God with purpose, power, and potential.

The Power of Discovering Your True Identity

When I finally started peeling back the layers of the mask I had been wearing for so long, it was tough. It wasn't easy to admit that the person I had been pretending to be—the guy who looked like he had everything under control—was just a front. But once I began to embrace my real identity in Christ, everything started to shift.

Here's the truth: when you discover who you really are, you get free. The inner man, the part of you that's connected to God, knows the truth. You are fearfully and wonderfully made (Psalm 139:14). You were created for more than just surviving. You were created to thrive.

The Bible says in John 8:32 (KJV), "And ye shall know the truth, and the truth shall make you free." That's what happens when you stop living behind a mask and start embracing the truth of who you really are. The chains of fear, doubt, and insecurity start to fall away, and you begin to walk in real freedom.

How This Connects to Recovery

If you've ever battled addiction, depression, or any kind of deep struggle, you know what it feels like to wear a mask. You get so used to pretending like you're fine, like you've got it all together, that it becomes second nature. But recovery isn't just about breaking the habit—it's about breaking free from the lies you've been telling yourself.

For me, the journey to recovery was also a journey to rediscover who I really was. I had to take off the mask of the person I thought I had to be—the one who was just trying to survive—and embrace the person God created me to be. That person is stronger than the addiction, bigger than the pain, and free from the past.

What You Can Do Right Now

If you're ready to start living in your true identity, here's how you can start peeling back the layers of the mask:

1. **Ask God to Show You Who You Really Are**
   Pray and ask God to reveal your true self. The person you've been hiding behind isn't who you are. Let God show you the person He created you to be.

2. **Let Go of the Old You**
   The outer man is the old you—the one shaped by the world. Start making decisions that reflect the new man. You don't have to live up to anyone else's expectations. Live in the truth of who you are in Christ.

3. **Speak Life Over Yourself**
   Stop speaking from your mask. Stop saying things like, "This is just who I am" or "I'll never change." Start declaring the truth of who you are in Christ. "I am a new creation." "I have a purpose." "I am not defined by my past."

4. **Walk in Confidence**
   Confidence isn't about pretending to have it all together. It's about knowing who you really are, even in the tough moments. Hold your head high, not because you're wearing a mask, but because you're walking in the truth of your identity.

Takeaway: The Mask is a Lie—The Real You is Free

Here's the truth: the mask is a lie. The person you've been pretending to be isn't who you are. The real you is stronger, smarter, and more powerful than you've been led to believe. But you'll never discover that person if you keep hiding behind the mask.

When you take off the mask and step into your true identity, you start living in freedom. And that freedom? It's the key to breaking free from addiction, from pain, and from everything that's been holding you back. It's time to stop pretending and start living in the truth of who you really are. The mask has served its time—it's time for the real you to rise.

Chapter 4

Destroying Strongholds

We've talked about the war between your inner man and outer man, the battle of the mind, and taking off the masks that have been holding you back. Now, let's get into something that most people don't even realize they're dealing with: strongholds.

A stronghold is something that's got such a tight grip on you that it feels impossible to break free. It's not just a bad habit or a negative thought—it's deeper than that. It's a mental, emotional, and spiritual block that keeps you stuck in a cycle of defeat. And the longer it's in place, the harder it becomes to tear down.

But here's the good news: no matter how big that stronghold feels, it can be destroyed.

What Is a Stronghold?

So, what exactly is a stronghold? In the Bible, a stronghold was a fortified place, like a castle or a city surrounded by walls. It was designed to keep things out and make sure nothing could get in. Spiritually speaking, a stronghold is something that's been built up in your mind and heart, trapping you inside and keeping you stuck in a cycle of defeat.

The Bible says in 2 Corinthians 10:4-5 (KJV), "For the weapons of our warfare are not carnal, but mighty through God to the pulling down of strong holds; Casting down imaginations, and every high thing that exalteth itself against the knowledge of God, and bringing into captivity every thought to the obedience of Christ."

Right there, it's telling us that strongholds are mental and spiritual barriers, and they go against the truth of who God says we are. These strongholds can be anything from addiction, fear, doubt, anger, or even self-hate. They're built up over time, brick by brick, thought by thought, and they get stronger the more we feed into them.

For me, my stronghold was addiction. I believed I couldn't live without it. I thought that was just the way my life was going to go. That belief had built up in my mind like a fortress, and every time I gave in, it got stronger. But here's the truth: strongholds don't stand a chance when you bring them into the light of God's truth.

How Strongholds Are Built

Strongholds don't show up overnight. They're built slowly, and most of the time, we don't even realize it's happening. It starts with a thought—something small, like "I'm not good enough," "I'll never change," or "This is just who I am." That thought grows into a belief, and that belief starts to control your actions, your decisions, and your life.

Before you know it, you're trapped in a stronghold.

Maybe for you, the stronghold is fear. Maybe it's anger or insecurity, or maybe it's that voice in your head telling you you'll never be more than what you've been through. Whatever it is, it didn't get there overnight. But the moment you recognize it for what it is—a lie—you can start tearing it down.

How to Destroy Strongholds

Here's the truth: strongholds might feel impossible to break, but they're not. The Bible tells us we have weapons that are stronger than any stronghold we face. These weapons aren't physical—they're spiritual, and they're mighty through God. When you use them, strongholds don't stand a chance.

Here's how you start tearing them down:

1. **Identify the Lie**
   Every stronghold is built on a lie. That's the foundation. The enemy knows that if he can get you to believe something that goes against God's truth, he's got you trapped. So, the first step is identifying the lie. What's the stronghold that's been holding you back? Is it addiction? Fear? Doubt? Anger? Recognize it for the lie that it is.

2. **Replace the Lie with Truth**
   Once you've identified the lie, you've got to replace it with truth. This is where God's Word comes in. The Bible is your weapon because it tells you the truth about who you really are. If your stronghold is fear, replace that lie with the truth that "God has not given us the spirit of fear; but of power, and of love, and of a sound mind" (2 Timothy 1:7, KJV). If your stronghold is addiction, replace that lie with the truth that "If the Son therefore shall make you free, ye shall be free indeed" (John 8:36, KJV).

3. **Take Every Thought Captive**

   This is where the battle happens—in your mind. Every thought that comes in that goes against God's Word? Capture it. Don't let it run wild. 2 Corinthians 10:5 (KJV) says, "bringing into captivity every thought to the obedience of Christ." That means when a thought comes in saying, "I'll never change," you don't entertain it. You capture it and replace it with truth. You tell yourself, "No, I am a new creation in Christ."

4. **Pray for Strength**

   You can't do this alone. Strongholds are spiritual battles, and that means you need spiritual strength to tear them down. Pray for God to give you the strength to recognize the lies, stand on His truth, and destroy the strongholds that have been holding you back. When you bring God into the fight, you're not fighting alone.

How This Connects to Recovery

If you've ever battled addiction, you know it feels like a stronghold. It feels like no matter how hard you try, you can't break free. And that's because addiction—like most strongholds—is rooted in a lie. It's the lie that you need that substance to survive. The lie that you'll never be anything more than the label the world has put on you.

But here's the thing: when I started breaking down the stronghold of addiction in my life, I realized it was built on that exact lie. And once I started replacing that lie with God's truth—that I had a purpose, that I was stronger than my addiction, and that I was free in Christ—that stronghold started to crumble.

It didn't fall overnight, but little by little, brick by brick, the walls came down. And it wasn't because I fought harder—it was because I leaned on God's strength and His truth.

What You Can Do Right Now

If you're ready to start tearing down the strongholds in your life, here's how you can start today:

1. **Identify the Stronghold**
   What's been holding you back? Is it fear? Addiction? Doubt? Anger? Recognize it for the lie that it is. Name it.

2. **Find the Truth**
   Once you've identified the lie, find the truth in the Bible that destroys that lie. If your stronghold is fear, start meditating on verses like "God is our refuge and strength, a very present help in trouble" (Psalm 46:1, KJV). If your stronghold is addiction, find verses that speak to your freedom in Christ.

3. **Take Your Thoughts Captive**
   Every day, take control of your thoughts. Don't let lies run loose in your mind. Capture them and replace them with the truth of who you are in Christ.

4. **Pray for God's Help**
   You don't have to fight this battle alone. Pray for God to give you the strength to destroy the strongholds in your life. And trust me—He will.

Takeaway: Strongholds Are Meant to Be Destroyed

Strongholds might seem impossible to break, but they're not. They're built on lies, and lies can't stand against the truth. When you bring God's Word into the fight, strongholds don't stand a chance.

You've got the power to destroy the strongholds that have been holding you back. It's not going to be easy, but every time you replace a lie with the truth, every time you capture a negative thought, you're tearing down those walls. And once those walls fall, you'll step into the freedom you were created for.

Chapter 5

Equipping Yourself with Spiritual Armor

We've been breaking down strongholds and talking about how to identify the lies that hold us back. Now, let's take it deeper by focusing on how to prepare yourself for the battle that's always raging within—the war between your inner man and your outer man. The thing is, it's not enough to simply knock down the walls of strongholds. You've got to be equipped to fight this ongoing war every day. You need the right tools to defend and protect yourself spiritually, because the outer man—the flesh—never stops trying to pull you back into your old habits.

So, how do you stay strong? How do you protect yourself from being dragged back into the same struggles? The answer is simple: you've got to put on your spiritual armor.

What is Spiritual Armor?

In Ephesians 6:11 (KJV), it says, "Put on the whole armor of God, that ye may be able to stand against the wiles of the devil." This isn't just a metaphor—this is real. Your spiritual armor is what protects you from the attacks the enemy throws your way, whether they're mental, emotional, or spiritual.

This armor isn't something you can physically see, but it's something you can feel when you put it on. It's the thing that keeps you grounded, keeps your inner man strengthened, and keeps your flesh from pulling you back into the cycle of defeat. Let's break down what this armor looks like and how you can use it to keep your spirit in control.

The Belt of Truth

First up, we've got the belt of truth. In Ephesians 6:14 (KJV), it says, "Stand therefore, having your loins girt about with truth." This is the foundation of your armor. The belt of truth holds everything together because it's all about walking in truth.

Remember how we talked about strongholds being built on lies? The belt of truth is what protects you from those lies. The more you know the truth about who you are, who God is, and what He has promised you, the less power the flesh has over you. The truth keeps you focused on feeding your inner man, not your outer man.

For me, the truth was my anchor. It was the truth that God created me for more than addiction, for more than temporary highs, and for more than the emptiness the world offers. When you know the truth, you stop chasing the things that drain your spirit and start living with purpose.

The Breastplate of Righteousness

Next, we've got the breastplate of righteousness. "And having on the breastplate of righteousness." (Ephesians 6:14, KJV)

The breastplate protects your heart, and righteousness means living in a way that's right with God. The more you feed your inner man through faith and right living, the more protected you are from the attacks of the outer man. The breastplate of righteousness guards your heart from being led astray by the temporary desires of the flesh.

When I was caught up in my struggles, my heart was wide open to anything that promised to numb the pain. The breastplate of righteousness taught me that guarding my heart wasn't about perfection—it was about aligning my life with God's will. The more I did that, the less power my outer man had over me.

The Shoes of Peace

"...and your feet shod with the preparation of the gospel of peace;" (Ephesians 6:15, KJV)

The next piece of armor is all about where you're walking. The shoes of peace protect you as you move through life. When your spirit is walking in God's peace, no matter what chaos is going on around you, you're stable. The outer man thrives on confusion, anxiety, and restlessness, but the inner man knows that peace comes from walking in alignment with God's purpose.

For years, I thought peace was something you found in a bottle or in success. But the real peace I found—the kind that truly strengthens the inner man—came from God. And once I had that peace, it didn't matter how wild life got. My inner man stood firm.

The Shield of Faith

"Above all, taking the shield of faith, wherewith ye shall be able to quench all the fiery darts of the wicked." (Ephesians 6:16, KJV)

Faith is your shield. This is what protects you from the attacks that come your way. Whether it's doubt, fear, temptation, or anything else trying to shake you, your faith blocks it.

Faith isn't just believing when things are good—it's trusting when things are hard. When the outer man is throwing every craving, every past hurt, and every lie at you, your shield of faith is what keeps you standing. Faith in God's promises keeps you from getting knocked down.

The Helmet of Salvation

"...and take the helmet of salvation." (Ephesians 6:17, KJV)

The helmet of salvation protects your mind. The outer man loves to mess with your thoughts—filling your head with fear, doubt, and confusion. But the helmet of salvation reminds you that your mind is guarded by the truth that you're saved, forgiven, and walking in victory. The enemy has no authority over you because you're covered by God's grace.

The Sword of the Spirit

Finally, we've got the sword of the Spirit, which is the Word of God. "And the sword of the Spirit, which is the word of God." (Ephesians 6:17, KJV)

This is your weapon. The Word of God isn't just something you read—it's something you fight with. Every time the flesh tries to pull you back, every time the outer man tries to take over, you use the Word to strike back. Jesus did this in the wilderness when He was tempted—He fought with scripture.

That's your sword. Every time temptation comes knocking, you respond with the Word. Every time fear tries to creep in, you hit it with the truth. Every time the lies of the outer man try to gain control, you use scripture to fight back.

How This Connects to Recovery

When you're fighting to stay free from addiction, the outer man will always try to pull you back. Old habits, old environments, old cravings—they'll all come for you. That's why you've got to be equipped. You need to wear your spiritual armor daily to protect your spirit and keep the flesh in check.

Recovery isn't just about breaking free from addiction—it's about staying free. And the only way to stay free is by protecting yourself with the armor of God. The more I suited up with truth, righteousness, peace, faith, salvation, and the Word, the more control my inner man had over my life.

What You Can Do Right Now

If you want to stay strong in your recovery and in your spiritual walk, here's how you can start putting on your armor every day:

- **Start with the Truth:** Every day, remind yourself of the truth. Who are you in Christ? What has God promised you? Let that truth be the foundation of your day.
- **Guard Your Heart:** Be mindful of what you allow into your heart. The breastplate of righteousness is about protecting yourself from the influences that try to pull you back into your old ways.

- **Walk in Peace:** No matter what chaos surrounds you, keep your spirit grounded in God's peace. Stay focused on your purpose, and don't let the distractions of the outer man shake you.
- **Use Faith as a Shield:** When doubt or temptation comes, hold up your shield of faith. Trust in what God has promised you, even when life gets tough.
- **Protect Your Mind:** Put on the helmet of salvation every day. Don't let the lies of the flesh or the world mess with your mind.
- **Fight with the Word:** Keep the sword of the Spirit close. Whenever the outer man tries to take control, hit it with scripture.

Takeaway: Stay Equipped for the Battle

The battle between your inner man and outer man is ongoing, and every day you need to be equipped for the fight. When you wear your spiritual armor, you're not just defending yourself—you're staying in control. You're feeding your spirit, and that's what gives you the strength to keep moving forward in victory.

Chapter 6

Stepping into Your Purpose

We've talked about the battles we face—strongholds, the war in the mind, and how to protect yourself with the armor of God. But here's the real game-changer: once you break free, once you start putting that armor on every day, it's time to step into your purpose.

Your purpose isn't just some far-off dream or something that only a few people are meant to find. You were created with a purpose. And once you find it, that's when life changes. That's when everything you've been through starts to make sense, and you begin to see why the battle was so intense—because the enemy was trying to keep you from stepping into your God-given purpose.

Why Purpose Matters

Purpose is what keeps you moving forward when life gets hard. It's the reason you get up in the morning. When you know why you're here, what God created you for, the struggles you face don't hit the same way. You see past the obstacles because you know that there's something bigger for you on the other side.

The Bible says in **Jeremiah 29:11 (KJV)**, "For I know the thoughts that I think toward you, saith the Lord, thoughts of peace, and not of evil, to give you an expected end." God's already got a plan for your life. He's got a purpose for you, and it's not just to survive—it's to thrive.

Finding Your Purpose in the Middle of the Struggle

When I was deep in my struggles, I couldn't see past the next day, let alone think about purpose. I was too busy just trying to survive. But here's what I realized: God was shaping me through all of it. Every battle, every struggle, every failure was leading me to the place where I could finally step into the purpose He had for me.

Sometimes we think our purpose is hidden, but the truth is, it's right there in front of us. It's in the things you're passionate about, the things that make you come alive. For me, part of my purpose is sharing my story, using my journey to help others break free. Your purpose might look different, but I can guarantee you this—God's already put it inside of you.

Romans 8:28 (KJV) says, "And we know that all things work together for good to them that love God, to them who are the called according to his purpose." That means even the things you've been through—the pain, the mistakes, the setbacks—God's gonna use it all for good.

Living on Purpose

Once you find your purpose, it's not enough to just know it—you've got to live it. That's where the real power comes in. Living on purpose means waking up every day and making choices that align with who you are and what God's called you to do. It means not letting the past or the mistakes define you anymore. It means stepping into your future with confidence, knowing that you're not here by accident.

Ephesians 2:10 (KJV) says, "For we are his workmanship, created in Christ Jesus unto good works, which God hath before ordained that we should walk in them." God created you for good works. He designed you with a purpose in mind, and once you start walking in that purpose, you'll see how everything begins to fall into place.

How to Start Walking in Your Purpose

So how do you start stepping into your purpose? How do you go from just surviving to living with intentionality? Here's how you can begin:

- **Pray for Clarity and Guidance:** Ask God to reveal your purpose. If you're not sure what it is yet, pray for clarity and guidance. Ask Him to show you what He's created you to do, and trust that He will guide you.
- **Pay Attention to What Moves You:** What are the things that light you up? What makes you feel alive? Your purpose is often tied to your passions. For me, it was telling my story, helping people, and sharing the things I've learned along the way. For you, it could be something different, but I promise—it's there.
- **Align Your Actions:** Once you know your purpose, start aligning your actions with it. Every day, ask yourself, "Is

what I'm doing right now helping me walk in my purpose?" If it's not, start making changes. Your purpose isn't some future goal—it's something you live out daily.

- **Overcome the Fear of Failure:** Stepping into your purpose can feel scary because the enemy knows how powerful you'll be once you do. Don't let fear hold you back. Remember, God's got you. He's already gone before you, and He's prepared the way.
- **Stay Focused on the Bigger Picture:** Life's gonna throw challenges at you, but when you're living with purpose, those challenges don't hit the same way. Stay focused on the bigger picture—the plan God has for your life. Let that keep you grounded, no matter what comes your way.

How This Connects to Recovery

When you're in recovery, finding your purpose becomes the thing that keeps you moving forward. It's not enough to just stop the destructive behavior—you've got to fill that space with something bigger. You've got to step into the reason why you were created.

For me, discovering my purpose wasn't just a nice idea—it was what saved my life. Once I realized that God had a plan for me beyond addiction, beyond the streets, beyond the mistakes, it gave me something to fight for. It gave me a reason to get up every day and keep pushing forward.

And it's not just about finding your purpose for yourself—it's about the impact you can make on others. Your story, your journey, your struggles—they're all part of something bigger. There are people who need to hear what you've been through because it'll help them get through their own battles.

What You Can Do Right Now

If you're ready to start living with purpose, here's how you can take the first steps:

- **Pray for Guidance:** If you don't know your purpose yet, ask God to reveal it to you. He's not gonna leave you guessing. Pray for clarity, and be open to what He shows you.
- **Find Your Passion:** What are the things that fire you up? What are the things that make you feel alive? Your purpose is often connected to the things you care about deeply.
- **Start Walking in It:** You don't have to wait until you've got everything figured out. Start living with purpose today. Make decisions that align with the person you're becoming, not the person you were.
- **Stay Consistent:** Living on purpose isn't a one-time thing—it's a daily choice. Stay consistent. Keep moving forward, even when things get tough. The more you walk in your purpose, the clearer it'll become.

Takeaway: Your Purpose Is Waiting for You

Here's the truth: you were created with a purpose. And once you start living in that purpose, everything changes. The struggles don't go away, but you see them differently. You realize that everything you've been through is part of the bigger plan, and you start moving with intentionality.

Your purpose isn't hidden—it's inside of you, waiting for you to step into it. And when you do? That's when you'll see just how powerful you really are.

Chapter 7

The Power of Perseverance

Alright, so we've talked about stepping into your purpose, living with intention, and letting God guide you. But here's the thing—just because you know your purpose doesn't mean life's going to get easier. In fact, sometimes it feels like the moment you step into your purpose, the challenges get even harder. That's why you need something powerful to carry you through those moments. That something is called perseverance.

Why Perseverance Matters

Life will always throw obstacles your way. There will be days when you feel like giving up, like nothing's working, and like the world is stacked against you. But perseverance? That's what keeps you standing when life tries to knock you down.

James 1:12 (KJV) says, "Blessed is the man that endureth temptation: for when he is tried, he shall receive the crown of life, which the Lord hath promised to them that love him." This verse reminds us that blessings don't come without trials. Perseverance means sticking it out through the tough times, trusting that there's a reward on the other side of the struggle.

Embracing the Struggle

Here's something I've learned: struggle is part of the process. There's no getting around it. But instead of letting it break you, you've got to learn to embrace it. Every time you're tested, every time you face an obstacle, it's an opportunity to grow stronger.

When I was battling addiction and trying to find my way out of the streets, there were so many times I wanted to quit. But here's what kept me going—knowing that every struggle was preparing me for the next level. The process wasn't easy, but it was necessary. It was shaping me into the person I needed to become in order to walk in my purpose.

Romans 5:3-4 (KJV) says, "And not only so, but we glory in tribulations also: knowing that tribulation worketh patience; And patience, experience; and experience, hope." That's the process right there—tribulation builds patience, patience builds experience, and experience builds hope. It's all connected.

How to Persevere When Life Gets Hard

Persevering through tough times isn't easy, but it's possible. Here's how you can keep moving forward, even when life tries to knock you back:

- **Stay Focused on Your Why:** When life gets tough, remember why you started in the first place. Remember your purpose. The enemy is always going to try to distract you and make you think you can't make it. But you have to stay locked into your "why." Why are you fighting? What's waiting for you on the other side of this struggle?

- **Trust the Process:** Perseverance is about trusting the process. You might not understand why things are happening the way they are, but trust that God is working behind the scenes. Every challenge is shaping you, preparing you for what's coming next.

- **Lean on God's Strength, Not Your Own:** There's a difference between trying to power through on your own and leaning on God's strength. When you try to do everything by yourself, you're going to burn out. But when you lean on God, you tap into a strength that never runs out. **Philippians 4:13 (KJV)** says, "I can do all things through Christ which strengtheneth me." That's the key—through Christ.

- **Celebrate the Small Wins:** Perseverance isn't just about pushing through the big battles—it's about celebrating the small victories along the way. Every step forward is progress. Every day you stay clean, every moment you resist temptation, every time you choose faith over fear—that's a win. Don't wait until you've "made it" to celebrate. Recognize the progress you're making, even if it's slow.

How This Connects to Recovery

Perseverance is everything in recovery. There's no such thing as an easy road to freedom. Every day is a battle, and some days are harder than others. But here's what you have to understand—setbacks don't mean you've lost. They're just part of the journey. The real victory comes when you choose to get back up after you've been knocked down.

In my own recovery, there were plenty of times I slipped up. I'd make progress, and then something would pull me back into old habits. But the key to perseverance is refusing to stay down. Every time I got knocked off course, I had to remind myself that I hadn't lost as long as I got back up and kept fighting.

Proverbs 24:16 (KJV) says, "For a just man falleth seven times, and riseth up again." That's what perseverance looks like. You're going to fall, but as long as you rise again, you're still in the fight.

Staying in the Fight

The enemy's goal is to make you feel like you've failed, like you've lost, like it's over. But as long as you're breathing, it's not over. You have the power to keep fighting, to keep moving forward, and to keep rising every time you fall.

One thing I've learned is that God doesn't ask for perfection—He asks for progress. And progress comes through perseverance. Every time you choose to keep going, you're growing. Every time you refuse to quit, you're getting stronger.

What You Can Do Right Now

If you're struggling to keep going, here's what you can do to start building perseverance:

- **Remind Yourself of Your Purpose:** Every morning, remind yourself of why you're fighting. Write it down if you have to. Your purpose is bigger than the struggle, and it's what's going to keep you moving forward.

- **Take It One Day at a Time:** Perseverance isn't about tackling everything at once. It's about taking it one day at a time, sometimes even one moment at a time. Focus on what you can do today, and let tomorrow take care of itself.
- **Surround Yourself with Support:** Perseverance isn't something you have to do alone. Surround yourself with people who will encourage you, who will pick you up when you're down, and who will remind you of your strength when you forget.
- **Keep Your Eyes on the Prize:** Every struggle, every setback, every hard day—it's all leading you to something greater. Keep your eyes on the prize, and don't let the temporary struggles take your focus off what's waiting for you on the other side.

Takeaway: Perseverance Is the Key to Victory

Here's the truth: perseverance is the key to victory. It's not about how fast you get there—it's about your willingness to keep going, no matter how many times you fall. Every battle, every challenge is building you up, making you stronger, and preparing you for the purpose God has for you.

Don't give up. Don't quit. Keep pushing, keep fighting, and keep rising every time life knocks you down. Perseverance is what separates those who survive from those who thrive.

Chapter 8

The Power of Community

W e've talked about the battle between the inner man and the outer man—the war between your spiritual self and the desires of the flesh. Now, we need to address one of the most powerful tools in winning this battle: community. Surrounding yourself with the right people is crucial because they can either feed your inner man or empower your outer man. Who you let into your life has the power to shape how you think, act, and ultimately, who you become.

The Role of Community in Strengthening the Inner Man

Your inner man—the spiritual side of you—needs constant support to thrive. When you surround yourself with people who are grounded in faith and focused on growth, they feed your spirit and help you resist the cravings and distractions that come from the outer man. This is where the power of community comes into play.

When I started to rebuild my life, one of the first things I had to change was the people I surrounded myself with. The crowd I used to run with wasn't helping me feed my inner man. They were keeping me stuck in the same cycle, feeding the desires of the flesh. The Bible tells us in Proverbs 13:20 (KJV), "He that walketh with wise men shall be wise: but a companion of fools shall be destroyed." I learned that if I wanted my inner man to grow stronger, I needed to walk with people who were wise, people who would build me up rather than drag me down.

The Power of Letting Go

Here's something you need to know: letting go of people, situations, or habits that are pulling you down isn't just a practical decision—it's an act of faith. By making changes in your life without acting in fear, you're demonstrating trust in God's plan for you. In 2 Timothy 1:7 (KJV), it says, "For God hath not given us the spirit of fear; but of power, and of love, and of a sound mind." When you move forward without fear, you're telling the world and yourself that you trust God to provide and guide your steps.

Sometimes, we're afraid to let go of what's familiar, even when we know it's hurting us. But the moment you take action—when you start removing the things in your life that are feeding the outer man—you'll witness spiritual things begin to happen right before your eyes. It's a sign of faith when you say, "I'm choosing the inner man over the outer man, and I trust God to take care of the rest." At that point, you can almost sit back and watch the changes unfold in real time.

Accountability and Support

A strong community holds you accountable. When you're in the heat of the battle, caught between what the inner man desires and what the outer man craves, you need people who will remind you of your purpose and hold you to the standard you've set for yourself. In Ecclesiastes 4:9-10 (KJV), it says, "Two are better than one; because they have a good reward for their labour. For if they fall, the one will lift up his fellow: but woe to him that is alone when he falleth; for he hath not another to help him up."

The right community will lift you up when you fall, but they will also challenge you to grow. They'll remind you that this battle isn't just physical or emotional—it's spiritual. You need people who understand that and who will push you to keep feeding the inner man, even when it feels like the outer man is winning.

Change Without Fear: A Leap of Faith

Changing the things in your life that are dragging you down without acting in fear is a sign of faith. It's easy to stay in familiar situations because we're afraid of what might happen if we step out in faith. But faith isn't about staying where you're comfortable. Faith is about trusting God enough to let go of the things that are feeding your outer man, even if it feels risky.

When you make that decision—when you say, "I'm done letting this hold me back"—that's when real change starts to happen. You're no longer just talking about faith—you're living it. And when you take that leap of faith, spiritual things begin to align. You start to see God working in ways you couldn't have imagined. You can sit back and witness it happening, live, right before your eyes.

This is the moment when the inner man begins to take over, and the outer man loses its grip.

How This Connects to Recovery

In recovery, community is essential. You need people around you who understand the battle between the inner and outer man, people who can remind you that your recovery isn't just about breaking old habits—it's about feeding your spirit. The right community will challenge you to keep growing spiritually, even when the outer man is trying to pull you back into old patterns.

In my own journey, I found that community wasn't just about support—it was about accountability. I needed people who weren't afraid to call me out when I was slipping and who would encourage me to keep feeding my inner man. This is why choosing the right people is so critical—they will help you stay aligned with your spiritual journey.

What You Can Do Right Now

If you want to start building a community that supports your inner man, here's what you can do:

1. **Evaluate Your Circle**: Take a look at the people around you. Are they feeding your inner man or encouraging the outer man? If they're not helping you grow, it might be time to make some changes.
2. **Find People of Faith**: Surround yourself with people who share your values and your faith. These are the people who will help you stay strong in your spiritual journey.
3. **Don't Be Afraid to Let Go**: Sometimes, the biggest act of faith is letting go of people or situations that are dragging you down. Trust that when you make that decision, God will take care of the rest.
4. **Get Accountable**: Find someone who will hold you accountable, who will push you to keep growing spiritually, and who won't let you slip back into old patterns.

Takeaway: Your Community Shapes Your Battle

The battle between the inner man and outer man is real, and it's one you can't fight alone. The people you surround yourself with will either help you win that battle or pull you down. But when you build a community that feeds your inner man, when you take action without fear and trust God's plan, you'll start to see spiritual transformation right in front of your eyes.

Let go of the things that are dragging you down and embrace the power of community to help you win the battle within.

Chapter 9

***

Mastering Self-Discipline

As we continue to explore the ongoing battle between the inner man and the outer man, one of the most important elements in this fight is self-discipline. The truth is, without self-discipline, even the strongest intentions will fall short. Mastering discipline is what allows your inner man to take control while keeping the outer man in check.

The Power of Self-Discipline

Self-discipline isn't about punishment or strict rules—it's about freedom. It's the freedom to choose what's best for your inner man, even when your outer man is screaming for instant gratification. It's the power to stay consistent in the choices that build your spirit and starve the flesh.

In 1 Corinthians 9:27 (KJV), Paul says, "But I keep under my body, and bring it into subjection: lest that by any means, when I have preached to others, I myself should be a castaway." Paul understood the need for discipline, recognizing that without it, the flesh can easily take over, no matter how well you start.

The outer man is all about indulging in what feels good now—whether it's chasing after addictions, distractions, or anything that feeds temporary pleasure. But the inner man thrives on long-term fulfillment and spiritual growth. That's why self-discipline is so powerful—it strengthens your spirit by teaching you to say "no" to the immediate cravings of the outer man and "yes" to the lasting rewards of the inner man.

Discipline in the Small Things

Discipline doesn't just show up in the big moments—it's built in the small, everyday decisions. It's waking up early to pray and spend time with God when you'd rather sleep in. It's choosing not to engage in conversations that stir up negativity, even when your emotions are pulling you in. It's staying focused on your goals, even when distractions are everywhere.

Self-discipline is like a muscle—the more you exercise it, the stronger it gets. You don't have to start with big, life-changing decisions—start small. Build discipline in the little things, and it will spill over into the bigger battles you face.

Overcoming the Flesh

The outer man thrives on comfort and convenience, but the inner man knows that true growth comes from stepping outside your comfort zone. Self-discipline helps you overcome the flesh by teaching you to prioritize what's good for your spirit over what's easy for your body.

In Romans 7:18 (KJV), Paul says, "For I know that in me (that is, in my flesh,) dwelleth no good thing: for to will is present with me; but how to perform that which is good I find not." He's acknowledging the constant battle between wanting to do the right thing and the struggle to actually do it. That's where discipline comes in—it bridges the gap between intention and action.

Self-Discipline in Recovery

Self-discipline plays a huge role in recovery. It's one thing to stop engaging in destructive behavior, but it's another thing to stay free from it. Discipline is what keeps you from going back to the things that once held you down. It's what strengthens your inner man and starves the outer man.

When I was in the early stages of recovery, it wasn't easy to stay on track. There were times when I wanted to give in to cravings, to go back to old habits, just to feel a sense of relief. But I knew that giving in would only feed my outer man and leave my spirit weaker than before. I had to choose self-discipline every day—sometimes every minute.

In recovery, self-discipline is about staying focused on the bigger picture. It's about choosing the long-term rewards of freedom and purpose over the short-term relief of old habits. And every time you make the right choice, your inner man grows stronger.

How to Build Self-Discipline

So how do you build the kind of self-discipline that strengthens your inner man and keeps the outer man in check? Here are a few key steps:

1. **Start Small**: Don't overwhelm yourself by trying to change everything at once. Pick one area where you want to build discipline, and start there. Whether it's spending more time

in prayer, cutting back on a habit that feeds your flesh, or focusing on positive thinking, start small and stay consistent.

2. **Hold Yourself Accountable**: Discipline thrives when there's accountability. Find someone you trust who can help you stay on track. Whether it's a friend, mentor, or someone from your community, having accountability keeps you honest with yourself and pushes you to keep growing.

3. **Stay Focused on Your Why**: Discipline is hard if you forget why you're doing it. Remind yourself of the bigger picture—why are you choosing to feed your inner man over your outer man? What's at stake? Keep your "why" front and center, especially when you feel like giving up.

4. **Celebrate Progress**: Don't wait until you've mastered discipline to celebrate. Every small step forward is a victory. Recognize the progress you're making, and use it as motivation to keep going.

The Spiritual Reward of Discipline

The reward of self-discipline is more than just feeling good about yourself—it's spiritual growth. Every time you choose discipline, you're choosing to build up your spirit and starve the flesh. You're strengthening your inner man and weakening the hold your outer man has over you.

Hebrews 12:11 (KJV) tells us, "Now no chastening for the present seemeth to be joyous, but grievous: nevertheless afterward it yieldeth the peaceable fruit of righteousness unto them which are exercised thereby." Discipline may not feel good in the moment, but the reward is peace, righteousness, and a stronger connection with God.

What You Can Do Right Now

If you're ready to start building self-discipline and feeding your inner man, here's what you can do today:

1. **Choose One Area to Focus On**: Pick one habit or area of your life where you want to practice more discipline. It could be your thoughts, your words, or your actions. Start small and be intentional.
2. **Stay Consistent**: Discipline is built through consistency. Even if you don't see results right away, keep going. Every time you choose discipline, you're making progress.
3. **Find Accountability**: Don't try to do it alone. Find someone who will encourage you and hold you accountable as you build discipline. This will help you stay on track when it gets tough.
4. **Trust the Process**: Building discipline takes time, but it's worth it. Trust that as you keep choosing to feed your inner man, your spirit will grow stronger, and the battle with the outer man will become easier.

Takeaway: Self-Discipline Strengthens the Inner Man

The battle between the inner man and the outer man is real, but self-discipline is your weapon. Every time you choose discipline, you're choosing to build up your spirit and weaken the flesh. It's a process, but with each step forward, your inner man becomes stronger, and your outer man loses its grip.

Remember, discipline isn't about perfection—it's about progress. And every small victory counts in the fight to live from your inner man.

Chapter 10

✦

Renewal is Powerful and Necessary

We've discussed the battles between the inner man and the outer man, but now it's time to dive into something that can reshape your entire life: **renewal**. Renewal isn't just a spiritual reset—it's about breaking old patterns, releasing negative influences, and replacing them with something greater. It's about dictating your own moves, not operating on the world's terms, and stepping into a life aligned with who you truly are, regardless of what society might consider "cool" or "trendy." Renewal is both powerful and necessary.

What Renewal Really Means

Renewal is about shedding the old, harmful patterns and embracing a new mindset that aligns with your true purpose. The world might accept or even encourage certain behaviors, but just because the world is fine with something doesn't mean it's good for you. I can tell you firsthand—the way I used to live, with a 40-ounce always in my hand, wasn't "cool" at all. But somehow, the world seemed perfectly fine with it. As adults, we need to be self-aware enough to stop worrying about what's trending and start focusing on what's right and what's wrong.

Renewal is about breaking away from those patterns. You have to stop performing for people who don't care about you and start living a life that aligns with your core values and beliefs. When you renew yourself, you reach a level of self-awareness that allows you to step away from the world's pressures and start living on your own terms. This isn't just a spiritual journey—it's a shift in how you view yourself and your purpose in the world.

Breaking the Pattern to Release Your True Self

Here's the thing about renewal: anything that breaks allows something new to emerge. When you break away from old habits, negative mindsets, or destructive behaviors, you create space for something better to take their place. While breaking these old patterns can be challenging, it's necessary for true renewal to happen.

Think of it like breaking a cycle. The outer man—the part of you tied to instant gratification, negativity, and the world's approval—has had control for too long. Renewal means freeing yourself from the chains that have been holding you back. There might be resistance from within and around you, but that's a sign that you're making real progress.

Renewing the Mind: Stepping Away from the World's Standards

A critical part of renewal is transforming your mind. The world will constantly try to tell you what's acceptable, what's popular, and how you should live your life. But when you renew your mind, you stop living by the world's standards and start living according to your true purpose.

Romans 12:2 (KJV) says, "And be not conformed to this world: but be ye transformed by the renewing of your mind, that ye may prove what is that good, and acceptable, and perfect, will of God." This renewal transforms you from the inside out, allowing you to step into a life that reflects who you really are. You're no longer chasing what the world says you should be—you're pursuing the life God has already ordained for you.

In my own life, I had to let go of the world's version of "cool" and embrace the reality of who I truly was. The process of renewal wasn't easy, but it was necessary. It allowed me to live with clarity, unaffected by the expectations of others.

Spiritual Renewal: Fueling Your Inner Man

Renewing your spirit is just as important as renewing your mind. Life can wear you down, especially when you're constantly battling between the inner man and the outer man. That's why spiritual renewal is crucial—it fuels your inner man and keeps you strong as you face the challenges of life.

Isaiah 40:31 (KJV) tells us, "But they that wait upon the Lord shall renew their strength; they shall mount up with wings as eagles; they shall run, and not be weary; and they shall walk, and not faint." Spiritual renewal gives you the strength to keep moving forward, even when the road is tough. It's not just a one-time thing—it's a daily choice to refresh your spirit and reconnect with your source of strength.

When you renew your spirit, you're no longer running on empty. You're not just surviving—you're thriving. Renewal allows you to regain your focus, clarity, and purpose. The inner man becomes empowered, making it easier to resist the pull of the outer man.

Renewal: A New Direction for Your Life

Renewal isn't just about refreshing your mind and spirit—it's about moving your life in a new direction. Breaking old patterns and embracing a new mindset isn't just a spiritual act—it's a bold, deliberate move that changes the course of your life. Renewal is about stepping away from what's holding you back and stepping into the purpose that's waiting for you.

When you make the decision to renew yourself, spiritual things start happening. You begin to see your life change in ways you never thought possible. You can sit back and watch your faith in action as God opens doors and creates opportunities you didn't see before.

The Bible tells us in 2 Timothy 1:7 (KJV), "For God hath not given us the spirit of fear; but of power, and of love, and of a sound mind." Renewal is a courageous act, one that requires you to move forward without fear. It's not just a reset—it's a total transformation in how you live, think, and view the world.

Renewal in Recovery: Breaking Free from the Past

For those in recovery, renewal is a vital part of the journey. It's not just about stopping a behavior—it's about renewing your entire approach to life. When you're in recovery, each day presents a new opportunity to break old patterns and embrace a new way of living.

I had to break free from the negative energy and destructive habits that were holding me back. The world didn't care if I stayed stuck in those patterns or if I broke free—but I had to care. Renewal allowed me to step into a new chapter of my life, free from the old ways of thinking and acting that were weighing me down.

In recovery, renewal is the process of choosing the inner man over the outer man, every single day. It's the decision to live with purpose and intention, rather than being controlled by the past.

How to Embrace Renewal Daily

So how do you live in renewal every day? Here's how to make renewal a part of your daily life:

1. **Break the Old Patterns**: Recognize the habits and mindsets that are holding you back. Don't be afraid to let them go, even if the world says they're okay. Renewal starts when you break the chains of old patterns.
2. **Renew Your Mind**: Feed your mind with truth, not the lies the world tells you. Spend time in God's Word, reminding yourself of who you are and what you're called to do. You don't need the world's approval—just God's guidance.
3. **Renew Your Spirit**: Take time each day to refresh your spirit. Whether it's through prayer, worship, or quiet reflection, make sure you're spiritually aligned and ready for whatever comes your way.
4. **Live with Courage**: Renewal requires boldness. It means stepping out in faith, without fear, and trusting that God's plan is bigger than any obstacle in your path.

The Rewards of Renewal

When you commit to renewal, you'll start to see the rewards. You'll notice a shift in your mindset, your energy, and your outlook on life. You'll begin to live with more purpose, more clarity, and more confidence.

Ephesians 4:23 (KJV) says, "And be renewed in the spirit of your mind." Renewal brings transformation from the inside out. It allows you to walk in alignment with your purpose, free from the old patterns that used to control you.

Takeaway: Renewal is Necessary for Transformation

Here's the truth: renewal is powerful, and it's necessary if you want to live a life of purpose and freedom. It's not just a spiritual reset—it's about breaking old patterns, moving in a new direction, and watching the transformation unfold before your eyes. You have the power to change your life, but it starts with the decision to renew your mind, your spirit, and your path.

When you commit to renewal, you're not just fighting the flesh—you're embracing a new way of living, free from fear and aligned with the person God created you to be.

Chapter 11

✦

Claiming Your Spiritual Authority

We've talked about renewal, self-discipline, and building a strong community. Now it's time to dive into a game-changer: spiritual authority.

Many people don't realize that they have the power to change their life not just by what they do but by the authority they have in Christ. If you're still feeling stuck, still battling the same struggles, it's time to recognize that God has already given you the authority to break free and walk in victory.

What is Spiritual Authority?

Spiritual authority isn't about controlling others—it's about knowing who you are in Christ and understanding that you have the power to overcome what's been trying to hold you down. The moment you put your faith in God, you were given authority over the things that used to control you—whether it's addiction, fear, depression, or doubt.

Luke 10:19 (KJV) says, *"Behold, I give unto you power to tread on serpents and scorpions, and over all the power of the enemy: and nothing shall by any means hurt you."* This isn't just symbolic; it's real power. God has already given you the authority to rise above any challenge the enemy throws your way.

Claiming Your Authority

You have to recognize and claim the authority God has given you. It's not enough to just know you have authority; you have to use it. Many of us walk through life feeling defeated because we're not tapping into the power that's already within us. It's like having keys to a locked door but never using them to open it. You've been given the keys—now it's time to unlock your spiritual authority.

Matthew 16:19 (KJV) tells us, *"And I will give unto thee the keys of the kingdom of heaven: and whatsoever thou shalt bind on earth shall be bound in heaven: and whatsoever thou shalt loose on earth shall be loosed in heaven."* The keys represent your authority in Christ. The struggles that have been binding you on earth can be broken when you step into this authority.

Using Faith as a Weapon

Your faith isn't just a comfort during hard times—it's your weapon in the fight. When the enemy comes at you with doubt, fear, or temptation, it's your faith that shields you.

Ephesians 6:16 (KJV) reminds us to *"Above all, taking the shield of faith, wherewith ye shall be able to quench all the fiery darts of the wicked."* The faith you hold is active and powerful, like a shield that blocks the lies and attacks of the enemy. When fear tries to blind you or hold you back, it's your faith that pushes you forward.

Faith is more than belief—it's action. It's stepping out in confidence, knowing God is guiding your steps. And with faith in your spiritual authority, you can move mountains.

Speaking with Authority

One of the most powerful ways to activate your spiritual authority is through your words. The Bible tells us that life and death are in the power of the tongue (Proverbs 18:21 KJV). What you speak over your life matters. If you constantly declare defeat—"I'll never change" or "I'll always be stuck"—then that's the reality you create.

But when you start speaking life over your situation—"I am free," "I am a new creation," "I walk in God's victory"—you are activating the authority God has already given you.

I've experienced this shift myself. When I stopped speaking defeat and started declaring victory, I began to see things change. I wasn't just speaking positive words—I was speaking with the authority of Christ, and that's when my circumstances began to transform.

Breaking Strongholds with Authority

When you step into your spiritual authority, you also have the power to break the strongholds that have kept you bound. Strongholds are mental, emotional, or spiritual blocks that try to keep you trapped in a cycle of defeat. These aren't just bad habits; they are deep-rooted barriers that require spiritual authority to overcome.

2 Corinthians 10:4 (KJV) says, *"For the weapons of our warfare are not carnal, but mighty through God to the pulling down of strongholds."* The power to break these strongholds doesn't come

from willpower alone—it comes from using the spiritual authority God has placed in you. It's understanding that you don't have to fight this battle on your own. You have divine power working through you.

Faith Without Fear

One of the biggest obstacles to walking in spiritual authority is fear. But 2 Timothy 1:7 (KJV) reminds us, *"For God hath not given us the spirit of fear; but of power, and of love, and of a sound mind."* When fear tries to creep in and blind your vision, remember that God has equipped you with power.

Changing the things in your life that are dragging you down without acting in fear shows that you're walking in faith. When you break old habits or remove toxic relationships without hesitation, you're demonstrating trust in God's plan. And when you step out in faith, you'll begin to see God work in ways you never thought possible.

How This Connects to Recovery

In recovery, spiritual authority is crucial. It's not just about willpower or breaking old habits—it's about stepping into the power God has already given you to overcome the things that once controlled you. When I realized that I didn't have to fight my battles alone, everything changed. I had the authority to speak freedom over my life, and I had the faith to act on it.

Recovery is more than just stopping destructive behaviors—it's about using your spiritual authority to declare a new life for yourself. This authority gives you the strength to not only stay free but to walk in victory every single day.

What You Can Do Right Now

If you're ready to step into your spiritual authority, here are a few ways you can start today:

- **Claim Your Authority:** Don't wait for someone else to tell you you have power—God has already given it to you. Start believing it and acting on it.
- **Speak with Authority:** Use your words to declare victory over your life. Speak freedom, strength, and purpose over your circumstances.
- **Use Faith as a Shield:** When doubts and fears come, stand strong in your faith. Trust that God has already equipped you with everything you need to overcome.
- **Break Strongholds:** Identify the strongholds in your life and declare them broken in Jesus' name. Pray with authority, knowing that God has given you the power to break free.

Takeaway: Walk in the Authority God Gave You

Here's the truth: you already have the authority to change your life. God has equipped you with the power to overcome every obstacle, break every stronghold, and walk in victory. But it's up to you to claim it.

You're not powerless, and you're not defeated. You've been given spiritual authority, and it's time to use it. Walk in that authority today, speak life over your situation, and watch as things begin to shift. This is your time to step into the power and purpose God has for you.

Chapter 12

---❖---

Vision - Seeing Beyond the Present

We've walked through self-discipline, spiritual authority, and the power of community. Now, it's time to discuss vision. Vision is more than just having goals or dreams. Vision is about seeing beyond your current situation and understanding the purpose God has for your life. Without vision, it's easy to get stuck, to feel like you're just going through the motions. But with vision, you have clarity, direction, and the ability to push through the obstacles that come your way.

What is Vision?

Vision is the ability to see beyond where you are now. It's not just about imagining a better future—it's about aligning with God's purpose for your life and seeing what He has in store for you. Proverbs 29:18 (KJV) says, *"Where there is no vision, the people perish."* Vision gives you life—it breathes purpose into everything you do and gives you the strength to keep moving forward, even when the path is hard.

But vision isn't something that just happens. You have to cultivate it, seek it, and align yourself with it. You need to be intentional about seeing what God wants for your life, rather than getting caught up in what the world says is important.

Aligning Vision with Faith

One of the biggest challenges in developing vision is aligning it with faith. It's easy to get stuck in what you can see right in front of you—your current struggles, limitations, or circumstances. But faith allows you to see beyond the present. Hebrews 11:1 (KJV) tells us, *"Now faith is the substance of things hoped for, the evidence of things not seen."*

Faith is what fuels your vision. Without faith, your vision is limited to what seems possible in the natural world. But with faith, your vision becomes limitless because it's grounded in what God can do, not what you can see right now.

When you align your vision with faith, you're no longer bound by the limitations of your present circumstances. You start to see possibilities where others see obstacles. You start to believe in outcomes that seem impossible to everyone else because you know God is in control.

The Power of Clear Vision

Having a clear vision is powerful because it gives you focus. When you know where you're going, it's easier to make decisions that align with that direction. It's easier to say "no" to distractions because you're clear on where you're headed.

Without clear vision, it's easy to get distracted, discouraged, and ultimately derailed. But when you have a clear sense of purpose, everything you do starts to line up with that vision. You begin to walk with intention, and even when challenges come, you stay focused because you know where you're going.

Vision Requires Action

It's not enough to just have vision—you have to act on it. Vision without action is just a dream. James 2:17 (KJV) says, *"Even so faith, if it hath not works, is dead, being alone."* If you have vision but never take steps toward it, that vision will never come to life.

You have to be willing to move in the direction of your vision, even when the path isn't clear. You have to take action, trusting that God will guide you as you step out in faith. The more you move toward your vision, the clearer it will become.

Sometimes, people get stuck waiting for everything to be perfect before they take action. But here's the truth: your vision doesn't need perfect conditions to come to life. It needs faith and action. Take the first step, even if it's small. Each step brings you closer to the vision God has for you.

Overcoming Obstacles to Vision

Every vision will face obstacles. Sometimes the biggest obstacle is fear—fear of failure, fear of the unknown, or fear of stepping out of your comfort zone. But remember, fear doesn't come from God. 2 Timothy 1:7 (KJV) reminds us, *"For God hath not given us the spirit of fear; but of power, and of love, and of a sound mind."*

Another obstacle is doubt—doubting whether you're capable or whether God's vision for your life is even possible. But God wouldn't give you a vision if He didn't also give you the ability to fulfill it. Ephesians 3:20 (KJV) says, *"Now unto him that is able to do exceeding abundantly above all that we ask or think, according to the power that worketh in us."*

When obstacles come, remember that they're part of the journey. They don't mean your vision is wrong—they mean you're moving in the right direction. Obstacles test your faith and your commitment, but they also strengthen your resolve. The key is to keep moving forward, trusting that God is with you every step of the way.

Vision and Community

Just like with spiritual authority, your community plays a huge role in your vision. The people you surround yourself with will either encourage your vision or discourage it. That's why it's so important to be intentional about who you let speak into your life.

Find people who will believe in your vision, even when it seems impossible. Find people who will encourage you to keep going when the path gets tough. Proverbs 27:17 (KJV) says, *"Iron sharpeneth iron; so a man sharpeneth the countenance of his friend."* The right community will sharpen you, challenge you, and push you toward your vision.

Vision in Recovery

In recovery, vision is crucial. Without vision, it's easy to get stuck in survival mode, just trying to make it through each day. But when you have a vision for your future—a vision of who you want to become, of the life you want to live—everything changes.

I remember when I first started my journey in recovery, I couldn't see past my struggles. It felt like every day was a battle just to stay afloat. But as I began to cultivate a vision for my life—seeing myself free from the chains of addiction, seeing myself walking in purpose—it gave me the strength to keep going. My vision gave me hope, and that hope fueled my recovery.

In recovery, your vision becomes your anchor. It's what keeps you grounded when the storms of life hit. It's what gives you direction when everything else feels uncertain. And the best part? Your vision isn't just about you—it's about the impact you'll have on the world once you're walking in your full purpose.

What You Can Do Right Now

If you want to start developing and acting on your vision, here are a few steps you can take:

- **Spend Time in Prayer:** Ask God to reveal His vision for your life. Spend time in prayer, seeking clarity and direction.
- **Write it Down:** Once you have a sense of your vision, write it down. Habakkuk 2:2 (KJV) says, *"Write the vision, and make it plain upon tables, that he may run that readeth it."* Writing your vision down helps you stay focused and gives you a tangible reminder of what you're working toward.
- **Take Small Steps:** Don't wait for everything to be perfect before you start moving toward your vision. Take small, actionable steps today.
- **Surround Yourself with Visionaries:** Find people who will support and encourage your vision. Let them speak life into your dreams and challenge you to keep going.

Takeaway: Vision is the Key to Moving Forward

Here's the truth: without vision, you'll feel lost. But with vision, you have purpose, clarity, and the strength to keep moving forward. Your vision isn't just a dream—it's the key to unlocking the life God has for you.

Don't let fear, doubt, or obstacles keep you from pursuing your vision. God has already given you everything you need to bring that vision to life. It's time to step out in faith, take action, and start seeing beyond the present.

Chapter 13

Inner Man Reclaims His Throne

In every person's life, there's a moment where the battle between the inner man and the outer man reaches its peak. It's a fight for control over who you truly are—the spiritual part of you that reflects God's will, versus the worldly part that's distracted by temporary pleasures. But before that battle even begins, we all start with something pure: the inner child. This inner child represents the spiritual innocence we were all born with, untainted by the world and full of trust in God.

The Innocence of the Inner Child

When we were young, life was simple. There was no baggage, no struggle for control between the inner and outer man. We came into the world with spiritual purity, a connection to God that was unclouded. Jesus Himself called us to return to that kind of faith and purity. In Matthew 18:3 (KJV), He says, *"Verily I say unto you, Except ye be converted, and become as little children, ye shall not enter into the kingdom of heaven."* The innocence of a child is what God desires from us—not just physical innocence, but a spiritual one. It's a state of complete dependence on God, where our hearts are open and trusting, free from the corruption of the world.

But as we grow older, the innocence of the inner child starts to fade. The world teaches us to rely on ourselves, to chase after things that satisfy the flesh—the outer man. This is when the battle begins. The inner man—the part of us that longs for God—gets pushed into the background, and the outer man starts to take over.

The Shift: From Child to Man

As we grow and experience life, the outer man begins to dominate. We face challenges, temptations, and distractions that pull us further away from the spiritual purity we once had. Paul speaks to this in 1 Corinthians 13:11 (KJV), *"When I was a child, I spake as a child, I understood as a child, I thought as a child: but when I became a man, I put away childish things."*

This scripture isn't just about physical maturity—it's about spiritual growth. The "childish things" we put away are the distractions, the temporary desires of the outer man that don't align with the will of God. As we grow, the inner man is supposed to take charge. But often, the opposite happens. The outer man—the part of us driven by pride, lust, and ego—takes the throne, and the inner man is pushed aside.

The Inner Man's Fight for the Throne

The inner man, representing your spiritual self, is constantly battling to reclaim the throne of your life. This is the part of you that understands God's purpose, that longs for peace, truth, and righteousness. But the outer man—the flesh—tries to keep that from happening. Galatians 5:17 (KJV) explains this struggle: *"For the flesh lusteth against the Spirit, and the Spirit against the flesh: and these are contrary the one to the other: so that ye cannot do the things that ye would."*

The flesh (outer man) and the Spirit (inner man) are in a constant war. The outer man seeks pleasure in temporary things—material success, physical gratification, the approval of others. The inner man seeks eternal things—connection with God, purpose, peace, and fulfillment. For too long, the outer man may have ruled your life, but now it's time for the inner man to reclaim his throne.

Reclaiming the Throne Through Spiritual Tools

We've discussed how the inner man, the spiritual you, can reclaim control over your life. But this battle isn't won through willpower alone. The tools you need are spiritual. 2 Corinthians 10:4 (KJV) says, *"For the weapons of our warfare are not carnal, but mighty through God to the pulling down of strong holds."* You can't fight the outer man with fleshly tools. You need the weapons God has given you—faith, prayer, and the Word of God.

- **Faith:** Faith is the foundation of your spiritual battle. Hebrews 11:6 (KJV) reminds us, *"But without faith it is impossible to please him: for he that cometh to God must believe that he is, and that he is a rewarder of them that diligently seek him."* Faith is what powers the inner man, keeping him connected to God and strengthening him for the battle ahead.

- **Prayer:** Prayer is your communication with God. It's not just about asking for help—it's about aligning your spirit with His will. Philippians 4:6-7 (KJV) encourages us: *"Be careful for nothing; but in every thing by prayer and supplication with thanksgiving let your requests be made known unto God. And the peace of God, which passeth all understanding, shall keep your hearts and minds through Christ Jesus."* Prayer equips the inner man with the peace and strength needed to withstand the attacks of the outer man.
- **The Word of God:** The Bible is the sword of the Spirit, and it cuts through every lie the enemy throws at you. Hebrews 4:12 (KJV) says, *"For the word of God is quick, and powerful, and sharper than any twoedged sword, piercing even to the dividing asunder of soul and spirit, and of the joints and marrow, and is a discerner of the thoughts and intents of the heart."* When the outer man tries to rise up, the Word of God reminds you who you really are and keeps your spirit anchored in truth.

Becoming Like a Child, But Walking as a Man

It's interesting that Jesus tells us to come to Him as a child, but Paul tells us to put away childish things. This isn't a contradiction—it's a spiritual truth. The innocence and purity of the inner child should guide our faith, but the maturity of the inner man should guide our actions. When you come to God, you come with the heart of a child—open, trusting, and fully dependent on Him. But as you walk in this world, you walk as a man—equipped with spiritual tools, ready to fight the good fight of faith.

The Inner Man Takes His Throne

Now is the time for the inner man to reclaim his rightful place. It's time to take back control from the outer man—the one who's been driven by selfish desires and temporary pleasures. Romans 8:5 (KJV) tells us, *"For they that are after the flesh do mind the things of the flesh; but they that are after the Spirit the things of the Spirit."* The inner man is after the things of the Spirit, and that's where true fulfillment lies.

Takeaway: Walking in Purpose Brings Fulfillment

In this battle between the inner man and the outer man, the victory belongs to the inner man. He's been fighting for you all along, and now, equipped with faith, prayer, and the Word of God, he's ready to take his rightful place. The outer man will always try to rise up, but with the spiritual tools God has given you, the inner man can remain on the throne, leading you in victory.

It's time to live as the person God created you to be—driven by faith, empowered by His Spirit, and walking in purpose. The inner man has reclaimed his throne.

Section 3

UNLOCKING DEEPER REALITIES

We're Going Deeper Now

So here we are. I told you from the start—we weren't just talking about **addiction** and **recovery**. We're going deeper than that. And if you thought the journey was gonna stop with me breaking down life on the streets, you're in for a surprise.

When I said we were going down the **rabbit hole**, I wasn't playing. You probably didn't think we'd end up talking about **quantum physics, other dimensions,** and how science backs up what the Bible's been saying all along. But that's exactly where we're headed. And trust me—it's not as far off as it sounds.

Let's keep it real for a second. Most people, when they think about **faith,** they think about it like some vague thing in the clouds, disconnected from the real world. But here's the truth: **science and faith are more connected than you think**. And the deeper I dug into both, the more I realized it's all part of the same story. God's story. **The Creator** is at the center of all of it.

Quantum Physics Isn't Just Theory

Now, let me be real with you. **Quantum physics** isn't just some abstract theory that only scientists understand. It's real. It's happening right now. They've already built a **quantum computer**—a machine that taps into **other dimensions**. Facts. This is what I've been learning, and it's blowing the doors off what most people think they know.

The same world you and I are living in is connected to worlds we can't see yet. This isn't sci-fi. This is **God's design**. When the Bible says in **Hebrews 11:3 (KJV)**, *"Through faith we understand that the worlds were framed by the word of God, so that things which are seen were not made of things which do appear,"* it's talking about **real stuff**. There are layers of reality we haven't even scratched the surface of, and faith gives us the ability to see beyond what's in front of us.

We're Gonna Look at It All

In this section, we're gonna look at the **science** and the **scripture**. We're gonna talk about **vibration**, **energy**, and how the universe works at its core. And you'll see that the Bible already gave us the keys to this knowledge. We're just catching up to what God's been telling us all along.

This isn't just about theory, and it's not about religion. This is about you learning how to use **faith** in ways you never thought possible. You've got more power than you think, and I'm about to show you how deep that power runs.

Chapter 1

The Double-Slit Experiment – Opening the Door to a New Understanding

Alright, so we've been through the struggle, right? You know my story. But now, I want to take you on a different kind of trip. We're about to go deep. And this ain't just about theory or some made-up stuff. This is real, and it's connected to everything I've been talking about.

So, let me hit you with this: have you ever heard of the **double-slit experiment**? Probably not, right? But don't trip, 'cause I'm about to break it down for you. This is where science, faith, and everything we've been learning about life comes together.

The Double-Slit Experiment: Breaking Reality Down

Imagine this: scientists shoot tiny particles—like light or electrons —at a barrier with two slits in it. Now, if no one's watching, these particles act like waves, spreading out and creating this pattern, like ripples on water. But the moment someone steps in and watches, the particles stop acting like waves. They act like solid little particles. The mere fact that someone is **watching** changes the way these things behave.

Now, you're probably like, "Yo, what does that even mean?" Let me tell you—it means that just **observing** something changes the outcome. Science has proven that the simple act of paying attention to something changes how it behaves. Think about that for a second.

What This Means for Us

This blew my mind when I learned about it. I had to stop and really think about it, 'cause it's deeper than just some scientific experiment. If particles change based on whether someone's paying attention, then what about us? What about our lives? The same rules apply.

What you focus on, what you put your energy and attention into—it changes everything. If science says just watching something can change the way it acts, what do you think happens when you start focusing on your life, your faith, your recovery? That's why when I started to pay attention to how I was living, and really put my focus on getting better, things started to shift.

Jesus Already Told Us This

You wanna know something even crazier? Jesus was already telling us this **thousands** of years ago. It's right there in the Bible. In **Matthew 17:20 (KJV)**, Jesus said, *"If ye have faith as a grain of mustard* *seed, ye shall say unto this mountain, Remove hence to yonder place; and it shall remove; and nothing shall be impossible unto you."*

Yo, that verse hit me differently after I learned about the double-slit experiment. Jesus wasn't just talking about moving physical mountains—He was talking about **faith** and **focus**. He was saying, "If you believe, if you put your mind and spirit on it, you can move anything in your life." The same way observing particles changes how they act, your faith can change how your life plays out.

How This Connects to Recovery

Now, I know we're all out here trying to move mountains. For some of us, that mountain is addiction, depression, broken relationships—whatever it is. But Jesus gave us the blueprint. You gotta have that faith, that belief, and focus.

When I was going through my recovery, I realized something: the more I focused on my past, the more stuck I got. But when I shifted my focus to my future, to what I could be, things started to move. I wasn't trapped in the same patterns. It's like those particles—what I was paying attention to was **shaping my reality**.

And trust me, I know it sounds crazy, but science is backing this up. It's showing us that our thoughts, our attention, and our faith have real power. You've got more control than you think. It's all about where you place your focus.

What You Can Do Right Now

Alright, so now that we're talking about focus and faith, what's next? What do you do with all this? Here's the key: start paying attention to what you focus on. Are you stuck on the negative? Are you trapped thinking about what went wrong? Or are you putting your energy into where you want to go?

Here's what you can do:

- **Shift Your Focus**: Start focusing on the future you want. Believe that it's possible. Whether it's kicking that addiction, healing your relationships, or just getting better—focus on that.
- **Build Your Faith**: Even if it's small, like that mustard seed Jesus talked about, let your faith grow. Start saying to yourself, "I'm moving forward. I'm not stuck." That little bit of belief is gonna go a long way.
- **Watch What Changes**: Once you start putting your attention on the right things, you're gonna see changes. Just like those particles, your life will start to shift. It's real, and it works.

Takeaway: You've Got the Power

So, if you take anything away from this, let it be this: you've got more power than you realize. Science is telling us that what we focus on changes things. Jesus has been telling us the same thing since day one. You've got the ability to move those mountains in your life—just focus, believe, and watch how reality starts to bend.

Chapter 2

Quantum Physics and the Power of Faith

Alright, let's keep this journey rolling. We already talked about how observation can change reality, but now we're gonna dive even deeper. We're gonna talk about something called **quantum entanglement**. I know it sounds wild, but trust me—by the end of this, you're gonna see how this connects to your life, your faith, and your recovery.

Quantum Entanglement: The Connection We Can't See

So, what is **quantum entanglement**? Imagine this: you've got two particles, right? Now, these particles can become **entangled**, which basically means they get connected. What's crazy is, no matter how far apart these particles are—whether they're side by side or on opposite sides of the universe—whatever happens to one particle instantly affects the other. It doesn't matter how far apart they are, they're always connected.

Now, you might be thinking, "Alright, that sounds cool, but what's it got to do with me?" Let me break it down for you. This concept of entanglement isn't just about particles—it's about **everything**. It shows us that everything in the universe is connected. And when I learned about this, I realized that this wasn't just science— it's the **truth of life** and faith.

Jesus Already Knew This

Here's the part that blew my mind: **Jesus** was already talking about this thousands of years ago. Check this out, in **John 15:5 (KJV)**, Jesus said, *"I am the vine, ye are the branches: He that abideth in me, and I in him, the same bringeth forth much fruit: for without me ye can do nothing."*

Now, think about that for a second. Jesus is saying that we're all connected to Him like branches to a vine. Just like those entangled particles, we're connected to Jesus and each other, no matter how far apart we seem. Everything is linked. You can't see it, but it's there, just like in quantum entanglement.

What This Means for Us

So, what does this mean for you and me? It means that **we're never really alone**. Even when it feels like we're isolated, when the struggle feels like it's ours to bear alone, we're still connected. We're connected to God, and we're connected to the people around us. Quantum entanglement shows us that what happens in one place affects another—just like in life.

When I was going through my recovery, I started to understand this on a deeper level. My actions weren't just affecting me. Every step I took toward healing was connected to my family, my friends, and my entire spiritual journey. Just like those particles, my choices were rippling out, touching everything and everyone around me, even when I couldn't see it.

Faith Connects Everything

This idea of connection doesn't stop with quantum physics. It's the core of faith. Jesus taught us that we are **one body**, united in Him. When we stay connected to Jesus, we're tapping into that power. We're tapping into the source that holds everything together.

And let me tell you—when I felt disconnected, like I was lost or too far gone to come back, I had to remember that I was **still entangled** with Him. I was still part of the vine. No matter how far I strayed, He was always connected to me, and I had the power to reconnect through faith. Colossians 1:17 (KJV): "And he is before all things, and by him all things consist."

How This Connects to Recovery

If you're reading this and thinking about your own journey, your own struggles, here's what you need to know: you're not in this alone. You're connected to something bigger than yourself, whether you can see it or not.

When I was deep in addiction, I felt like I was trapped in my own world, like nothing I did mattered. But the truth is, every step I took toward healing was connected to my loved ones, to the people who cared about me, and to my future self. **Every positive move** I made was sending ripples out into the universe, into my family, my friendships, and my relationship with God.

That's why when you make a decision to get better, it's not just for you. It's for the people you love, the people who need you. It's for your future. You might not see how it all connects right now, but believe me—it does.

What You Can Do Right Now

So, how can you use this understanding of connection in your life, in your recovery? Here's what worked for me:

- **Stay Connected to God**: No matter what you're going through, stay connected to the source. Just like Jesus said, *"I am the vine, ye are the branches."* When you stay connected to Him, you stay tapped into that power.
- **Remember the Ripple Effect**: Every choice you make sends ripples out into the world. When you choose to get better, you're impacting more than just yourself. You're changing the lives of the people around you, even if you can't see it.
- **Trust the Process**: Even when you feel like you're making small steps, trust that those steps are connected to a bigger picture. Just like in quantum entanglement, everything is linked, and your healing is part of a greater journey.

Takeaway: You're Never Alone

Here's the bottom line: you're not alone in this. You're connected—physically, spiritually, and emotionally. Science is telling us that everything in this universe is linked, and Jesus has been telling us that from the start. You've got the power to stay connected, to heal, and to move forward, not just for yourself but for everyone connected to you. So, don't ever feel like you're out here on your own. You're part of something bigger, and your faith is the key to tapping into that connection. Every step you take toward healing is a step toward reconnecting with the power that holds the whole universe together. There are several scriptures in the **KJV** that convey the idea of **Jesus holding things together** or being the sustaining force behind all creation and life. Here are some key passages that reinforce this concept beyond the "vine and the branches" analogy:

1. Hebrews 1:3 (KJV):
- "Who being the brightness of his glory, and the express image of his person, and upholding all things by the word of his power, when he had by himself purged our sins, sat down on the right hand of the Majesty on high." This verse speaks of Jesus as the one who upholds all things by the power of His word. It emphasizes His role in sustaining the universe and everything in it by His divine authority.

2. John 1:3 (KJV):
- "All things were made by him; and without him was not any thing made that was made." This scripture emphasizes that everything was created through Jesus. It implies that nothing exists outside of His creative power, and He is essential to the existence and continuation of all things.

3. Ephesians 1:22-23 (KJV):
- "And hath put all things under his feet, and gave him to be the head over all things to the church, Which is his body, the fulness of him that filleth all in all." This passage speaks to Jesus being the head over all things, particularly in relation to the church, but also in a broader sense, pointing to His role in governing and holding all things in place.

4. 1 Corinthians 8:6 (KJV):

- "But to us there is but one God, the Father, of whom are all things, and we in him; and one Lord Jesus Christ, by whom are all things, and we by him." This verse reinforces the idea that all things exist through Jesus and are held together by Him. It speaks of His sovereignty and the fact that everything owes its existence to Him.

5. Revelation 4:11 (KJV):

- "Thou art worthy, O Lord, to receive glory and honour and power: for thou hast created all things, and for thy pleasure they are and were created." While this verse does not specifically mention Jesus by name, it refers to the Lord as the Creator of all things, underscoring the idea that creation exists by His will and is held together for His purposes.

Chapter 3

Manifestation and the Creative Power of Faith

Alright, so now that we've talked about how everything is connected, we're about to level up even further. Let's get into something that's all around us but most people never even think about: **vibration**. I know, it sounds like some sci-fi stuff, but it's real. Everything—and I mean **everything**—is made up of energy that's vibrating. And the crazy part? Jesus was already dropping knowledge about this long before science caught up.

String Theory and Vibration: The Universe Is Energy

So, what's this vibration stuff all about? It comes down to something called **string theory**. Now, don't get lost in the big words—I'll keep it simple. String theory says that everything in the universe, from the biggest planets to the tiniest particles, is made up of **tiny, vibrating strings of energy**. These strings are so small you can't see them, but they're the building blocks of everything.

You, me, the chair you're sitting on, the phone in your hand—it's all vibration. Everything is energy, and the frequency at which something vibrates determines what it looks like, feels like, and acts like.

What This Means for Us

So why does this matter? Because **you're** vibrating too. Your thoughts, your words, and your actions—they all have a vibration. And that vibration is sending out energy into the world. What you put out is what you get back. That's why your mindset, your words, and your faith are so important.

When I was learning about this, I realized something: **what I was saying and thinking** was creating the world around me. If I kept speaking negative things—telling myself I was stuck, telling myself I'd never change—I was putting out that negative energy, and it was coming right back to me. I was shaping my world with my words, and I didn't even realize it.

Jesus Was Already Teaching Us This

Now, here's the part that'll blow your mind: **Jesus** was already talking about this long before any scientist started talking about string theory or vibration. He was dropping truth bombs about the power of our words and how they create the world around us.

In **Proverbs 18:21 (KJV)**, it says, *"Death and life are in the power of the tongue: and they that love it shall eat the fruit thereof."* Think about that. **Death and life**—the ultimate forces—are in your tongue, in what you speak.

When Jesus said this, He was telling us that our words carry real power. They're not just sounds we make—they're **vibrations** that shape reality. Just like string theory shows that everything is made of vibration, Jesus was teaching us that our words create life or death in our world. Every word you speak sends out a vibration, and it either brings life or destruction.

How This Connects to Faith

So, what's the connection between vibration and faith? It's simple: your **faith** is the energy behind your words. When you speak something in faith, you're putting out a high vibration—something that can create change. But if you're speaking doubt, negativity, or fear, you're putting out low vibrations that bring nothing but more pain and struggle.

Jesus showed us the power of words and faith over and over again. In **Mark 11:23 (KJV)**, He said, *"For verily I say unto you, That whosoever shall say unto this mountain, Be thou removed, and be thou cast into the sea; and shall not doubt in his heart, but shall believe that those things which he saith shall come to pass; he shall have whatsoever he saith."*

That right there? That's manifestation. That's using your words, powered by faith, to **move mountains**. And trust me, that mountain doesn't have to be made of stone. It could be addiction, depression, whatever's holding you back—when you speak to it with faith, you're sending out vibrations that **change reality**.

How This Connects to Recovery

When I was deep in my struggles, I didn't realize how much I was **speaking death** over my life. I kept saying things like, "I'll never change," "This is just who I am," and "There's no way out." Those words had power, and they were keeping me trapped.

But the moment I started to **speak life**—even when I didn't feel it yet—I began to see things shift. I started saying, "I'm getting better," "I'm breaking free," and "God has a plan for me." And those words, powered by my faith, started changing the way I saw myself and the way my life was playing out.

I began to realize that my words were creating the reality I was living in. The same way string theory says everything is made of vibration, Jesus was telling us that **our words are energy**, and that energy is either building us up or tearing us down.

What You Can Do Right Now

So, what can you do with all this knowledge about vibration, faith, and words? Here's the deal: you've got to start being **intentional** with what you say and think. You're putting out energy all the time, and that energy is shaping your world. Here's how you can flip the script:

1. **Watch Your Words**: Start paying attention to what you're saying about yourself and your situation. Are you speaking life, or are you speaking death? Remember, every word is sending out a vibration.
2. **Speak in Faith**: Even if you're not where you want to be yet, start speaking as if you are. Say things like, "I'm healing," "I'm growing," "I'm breaking free." Your words will start to bring that reality into existence.
3. **Believe in the Power of Your Words**: Don't just say it—**believe it**. When Jesus said you can move mountains, He wasn't playing around. The power is real, but it only works if you believe it in your heart.

Takeaway: Speak Life, Create Life

Here's the bottom line: you have the power to create life or death with your words. The same way everything in the universe is made of vibration, your words are sending out energy that shapes your reality. Jesus knew this. Science confirms this. And now, you know it too.

If you want to change your life, start by changing your words. Speak life, speak healing, and watch how the vibrations you put out start to shift everything around you. You're more powerful than you think, and your words are the key to unlocking that power.

Chapter 4

The Mind as a Tool for Recovery

Alright, we've already touched on how everything in the universe is connected and how your words are powerful vibrations shaping your reality. Now, we're about to get even deeper—into the **mind**. This chapter is all about how your brain works and how you can **reprogram it** to help you heal, grow, and transform your life. Sounds wild, right? But trust me, this is real.

Neuroplasticity: Rewiring Your Brain

So let's talk about this thing called **neuroplasticity**. Basically, it's the ability of your brain to **rewire** itself. Your brain isn't stuck in one way of thinking or behaving. It's constantly changing based on what you focus on, what you repeat, and what you believe.

Think of it like this: your brain is full of paths, right? The more you walk down a certain path, the more **worn-in** it gets, and the easier it becomes to take that path again. So if you're used to thinking negatively, if you're used to feeling stuck, your brain builds those paths to make it easier to stay there. But here's the kicker—**you can build new paths**.

Your brain can literally **rewire itself** based on your thoughts, actions, and beliefs. This is how habits are formed and how they're broken. Science has proven this. You're not stuck with the brain you have right now. You've got the power to **reshape** it.

Jesus Was Teaching Us This All Along

Now, here's where it gets even deeper: this concept of rewiring your brain isn't new. It's been in the **Bible** all along. In **Romans 12:2 (KJV)**, it says, *"And be not conformed to this world: but be ye transformed by the renewing of your mind, that ye may prove what is that good, and acceptable, and perfect, will of God."*

That's **neuroplasticity** right there—Jesus was telling us to **renew our minds**. He was telling us that we have the power to **transform** ourselves by changing the way we think. This isn't just about thinking positive thoughts; it's about literally rewiring your brain to support your growth, your healing, and your purpose.

How This Works in Real Life

Alright, let me break it down even further. In my own life, I was trapped in certain patterns of thinking for years. Addiction had me locked into a mindset where I believed I couldn't change, I couldn't get better, and this was just who I was. My brain had built up these paths so strong that I couldn't see any way out.

But when I started learning about **neuroplasticity**, and when I dug deeper into what the Bible was saying about **renewing my mind**, I realized that I didn't have to stay trapped. I started working on **rewiring my thoughts**. It wasn't easy, and it didn't happen overnight, but little by little, I started building new pathways in my brain.

I replaced the old negative thoughts with new ones:

- "I'm not stuck—I'm growing."
- "I'm not broken—I'm healing."
- "I'm not defined by my past—I'm creating my future."

And as I did that, my brain started to **change**. I could literally feel myself shifting from being trapped in my old ways of thinking to **opening up** to new possibilities.

The Power of Repetition and Focus

Here's the key: just like with anything in life, **repetition** is what makes the change happen. Your brain needs to keep walking down those new paths in order for them to get stronger. That's why you've got to stay focused on the **positive**, on the future you want, and on what God's Word says about you.

Every time you think a new thought, every time you speak a positive word, you're building a new path in your brain. And the more you walk that path, the easier it gets. That's how **neuroplasticity** works, and it's how **faith** works too. It's not just about believing once—it's about believing **over and over** until it becomes part of who you are.

How This Connects to Recovery

If you're in recovery, whether it's from addiction, depression, or anything else, this is huge. You might feel like you're trapped in the same cycle, like your brain is wired to keep you in that dark place. But I'm here to tell you—it doesn't have to be that way.

You've got the power to **rewire your brain**. You've got the power to **renew your mind**. And when you do that, you're going to start seeing changes in your life that you never thought were possible.

For me, rewiring my brain meant breaking free from the lies I'd been telling myself for years. It meant replacing those old thoughts with **God's truth**:

- "I am fearfully and wonderfully made." (Psalm 139:14)
- "I can do all things through Christ who strengthens me." (Philippians 4:13)
- "I am more than a conqueror." (Romans 8:37)

As I started repeating those truths, my brain began to shift. My old thoughts didn't have the same power over me anymore, and I began to **transform** into the person I was always meant to be.

What You Can Do Right Now

Here's how you can start rewiring your brain today:

1. **Focus on the Positive**: Stop letting negative thoughts run your life. Start focusing on the future you want, the person you're becoming, and the truth of what God says about you.
2. **Speak Life Over Yourself**: Just like we talked about in the last chapter, your words are powerful. Start speaking positive, life-giving words over yourself. Repeat them until they become part of who you are.
3. **Repetition Is Key**: This isn't a one-time thing. You've got to keep walking down those new paths in your brain. Every time you choose a positive thought over a negative one, you're strengthening those new pathways.

4. **Trust the Process**: It's not going to happen overnight. But the more you focus, the more you repeat, the more your brain will start to change. And as your brain changes, so will your life.

Takeaway: Your Mind Is the Key

Here's the truth: your mind is the most powerful tool you have in your recovery. And you've got the power to **renew** it, to **reprogram** it, and to **reshape** it. Jesus was telling us this all along—He knew that the way we think shapes the way we live.

Science is just now catching up with what the Bible has been saying for thousands of years. You're not stuck with the brain you have now. You can change it. You can grow. You can transform. It all starts with what you think, what you focus on, and what you believe.

Chapter 5

--- ✦ ---

Quantum Computers and Other Dimensions – A Glimpse Beyond

Alright, so we've been talking about how your words, your thoughts, and your faith are shaping your reality. Now, we're about to take it even further. Let's talk about something that's gonna push the limits of what most people think is possible: **quantum computers** and the idea of **other dimensions**. Yeah, we're going there.

Quantum Computers: Accessing the Unseen

First off, what's a **quantum computer**? I'm not talking about the laptop you use to stream Netflix or check Instagram. This is a whole different level. A **quantum computer** operates using the principles of **quantum mechanics**, which is the science of how things work at the smallest levels—down to particles smaller than atoms. These computers aren't like regular computers—they can process information in ways that **tap into other dimensions**.

Sounds crazy, right? But this is real. Quantum computers are out here right now, doing things that don't seem possible by the laws of physics that most of us are familiar with. They're proving that there's more going on than what we can see with our eyes.

The Bible's Been Telling Us This

Now, I want to tie this back to something the Bible says. In **Hebrews 11:3 (KJV)**, it says: *"Through faith we understand that the worlds were framed by the word of God, so that things which are seen were not made of things which do appear."*

That verse right there is deep. It's saying that **what we see is made from what we can't see**. The Bible is already talking about **unseen dimensions**, things that exist but aren't visible to us. And that's exactly what quantum mechanics and quantum computers are showing us—they're giving us access to things that are real but can't be seen in the traditional sense.

When I read that verse and started learning about quantum physics, it hit me hard. We've been taught that reality is just what's in front of us, but the Bible—and now science—are telling us there's more out there. There are **worlds**, dimensions, and realities that we can't see with our natural eyes.

How This Connects to Faith

Here's where it all comes together: **faith** is the bridge between what we see and what we don't see. Just like **Hebrews 11:1 (KJV)** says, *"Now faith is the substance of things hoped for, the evidence of things not seen."* Faith is what gives us access to the unseen, just like quantum computers are giving scientists access to dimensions beyond our reach.

You see, faith isn't just about believing in what's possible in this world—it's about tapping into the power of **God's creation**, which includes things we can't even imagine yet. When we operate in faith, we're not limited by what's in front of us. We're reaching into the **unseen**, into the dimensions where God is already working.

The Power of Other Dimensions

Now, let me be clear—I'm not talking about some sci-fi movie plot. When I say **other dimensions**, I'm talking about the realities that exist beyond what we can see with our eyes but are still part of God's creation. Think about it: the Bible already tells us that God exists outside of time and space. So why wouldn't there be layers of reality we can't see yet?

When Jesus performed miracles, He wasn't bound by the physical laws of this world. He was accessing the **supernatural**, the parts of creation that we don't fully understand yet. And here's the thing—through faith, we can tap into that same power. We don't need a quantum computer to access other dimensions. We've got **faith**, and that's more powerful than any technology could ever be.

How This Connects to Recovery

So how does all this tie into your life and your recovery? It's simple. **Faith** allows you to reach beyond what you can see right now. You might be looking at your situation and thinking, "There's no way out. This is just how it's gonna be." But that's only because you're seeing the world with **natural eyes**. Faith lets you look beyond that—into the dimensions where **God is working things out**, where miracles are possible, and where healing is already happening.

When I was deep in my struggle, I could only see what was in front of me—the addiction, the pain, the mistakes. But when I started to tap into **faith**, I realized that my situation wasn't the end. There was more happening that I couldn't see, and God was working in those unseen places to bring me out of the mess I was in.

That's why faith is so important in your recovery. It lets you tap into the power that exists beyond your current reality. Just because you can't see the way out doesn't mean it's not there. Faith gives you the ability to access the unseen, where God is already moving mountains on your behalf.

What You Can Do Right Now

So, how do you use this understanding of **other dimensions** and **faith** in your life? Here's what you can start doing right now:

1. **Activate Your Faith**: Start believing that there's more happening than what you can see. Just because your situation looks impossible doesn't mean it is. God is working in ways you can't see yet.
2. **Pray with Expectation**: When you pray, don't just ask for small things. Pray with the expectation that God is doing **big things** behind the scenes, even in dimensions you can't see.
3. **Trust in the Unseen**: Remember, the Bible tells us that what we see was made from what we can't see. Trust that God is using the unseen parts of His creation to bring about the breakthrough you need.

Takeaway: Faith Gives You Access to the Unseen

Here's the bottom line: **faith** is your key to accessing what you can't see. Just like quantum computers are tapping into other dimensions, your faith lets you tap into the **power of God's creation** beyond what's visible. The Bible has been telling us this all along—there's more going on than what meets the eye.

You've got the power to connect with the unseen, to reach beyond your current situation, and to access the blessings, healing, and freedom that God has already set in motion for you. Don't limit yourself to what you can see. Your faith is the gateway to a whole new reality.

Chapter 6

The Unseen Realities and Mighty Things

Alright, we've been on this ride together, and I told you from the jump we were going down the rabbit hole. I bet when I first said that, you didn't think we'd be diving **this deep**. But here we are—talking about the power of words, quantum physics, unseen dimensions, and how **faith** ties it all together. And if you're still with me, that means you're ready. Ready to take all this knowledge and use it to shape your life, your recovery, and your future.

I Told You He'd Show Us Mighty Things

Remember when I hit you with that verse from **Jeremiah 33:3 (KJV)**: *"Call unto me, and I will answer thee, and show thee great and mighty things, which thou knowest not."*?

Well, here we are. We've seen things that most people don't even think about. We've unlocked the power of **faith**, we've explored **quantum realities,** and we've tapped into the **vibration** that holds everything together. And the crazy part is—this is just the beginning. God's creation is so vast, so deep, that we're just scratching the surface of what's possible.

It All Comes Back to Faith

At the end of the day, it all comes back to **faith**. Faith is the key that unlocks every door. It's the bridge between the **seen and unseen**, the **known and unknown**. It's what allows you to step into your power and reshape your life.

You might be thinking, "Alright, Juice, I get it—but what do I do now?"

Here's what you do: **you use what you've learned**.

You start speaking life over yourself. You start rewiring your mind. You start believing in the things you **can't see yet**—the dimensions of God's creation that are already working in your favor. You start living by **faith**, knowing that even when you can't see it, God is moving behind the scenes.

The World Is Bigger Than You Think

If there's one thing I want you to take away from all of this, it's that the world is bigger than you think. Your reality is bigger than you think. And the power you have through **faith** is bigger than you think. You're not limited by what you see. You're not stuck in one place. You have access to the **unseen**, to the **great and mighty things** that God has waiting for you.

Your Journey Continues

This is your journey now. I've shared my story, my struggles, and the things I've learned along the way. But this is just the beginning for you. You've got the tools. You've got the knowledge. And most importantly, you've got the **faith**.

So when you leave here, don't leave empty-handed. Take everything we've talked about, put it into practice, and **watch your world change**. I'm not saying it's gonna be easy. I'm saying it's gonna be **possible**. Because now you know that with God, **all things are possible**.

Let's Bring It Home

Let me end it with this: **Jeremiah 33:3** wasn't just a promise to me—it's a promise to you. God is telling you that if you call on Him, He will **answer you**. He will show you things you've never imagined. But you've gotta be willing to take that step, to go down that rabbit hole of faith, and to trust that the unseen is just as real as what's right in front of you.

You've got the power. You've got the faith. And now it's time to use it. Well, its been real. If you made it this far then stop by and check up on me Sometimes, my YouTube channel is Quit Drinking With Bible. Good Luck.

Section 4

SPIRITUAL TOOLKIT: SCRIPTURES FOR EVERY STRUGGLE

Introduction

This toolkit is designed to provide scriptural encouragement for various life struggles. Whether you are battling addiction, searching for strength, or seeking hope, these verses can guide and uplift you. Turn to these passages when you need God's Word to light your path. May they be a refuge for you as you navigate life's challenges.

1. Overcoming Addiction and Temptation

When temptation comes knocking, these scriptures remind us that God offers a way out.

- **1 Corinthians 10:13 (KJV)**: "There hath no temptation taken you but such as is common to man: but God is faithful... will also make a way to escape, that ye may be able to bear it."
- **James 4:7 (KJV)**: "Submit yourselves therefore to God. Resist the devil, and he will flee from you."

Reflection: When temptation arises, where can you look for strength? How can you submit your struggle to God and resist the pull of addiction?

2. Strength for Difficult Times

In moments of weakness or despair, these verses provide comfort and reassurance that God is always present to offer strength.

- **Isaiah 41:10 (KJV)**: "Fear thou not; for I am with thee: be not dismayed; for I am thy God: I will strengthen thee."
- **Psalm 34:17-18 (KJV)**: "The righteous cry, and the LORD heareth, and delivereth them out of all their troubles."

Reflection: When life feels overwhelming, how can you remind yourself of God's promise to strengthen and uphold you?

3. Faith and Trust in God

Trusting God in all things is a pillar of the Christian faith. These scriptures reinforce the importance of fully placing our confidence in Him.

- **Proverbs 3:5-6 (KJV):** "Trust in the LORD with all thine heart; and lean not unto thine own understanding."
- **Matthew 17:20 (KJV):** "If ye have faith as a grain of mustard seed, ye shall say unto this mountain, Remove hence... and it shall remove."

Reflection: In what areas of your life can you release control and fully trust God's plan?

4. Personal Transformation and Renewal

These passages remind us of the power of God to renew our hearts and minds as we grow in faith.

- **Romans 12:2 (KJV):** "Be not conformed to this world: but be ye transformed by the renewing of your mind."
- **2 Corinthians 5:17 (KJV):** "If any man be in Christ, he is a new creature: old things are passed away; behold, all things are become new."

Reflection: How can you allow God to transform your thoughts and renew your mind daily?

5. Facing Fear and Anxiety

When fear and anxiety take over, these scriptures remind us of God's peace, which surpasses all understanding.

- **Philippians 4:6-7 (KJV):** "Be careful for nothing; but in every thing by prayer and supplication... the peace of God... shall keep your hearts and minds."

- **Psalm 56:3-4 (KJV)**: "What time I am afraid, I will trust in thee."

Reflection: How does prayer help calm your fears and bring peace into your life?

6. Guidance and Wisdom

For moments of uncertainty, these verses show that God is always ready to guide us when we seek His wisdom.

- **James 1:5 (KJV)**: "If any of you lack wisdom, let him ask of God... and it shall be given him."
- **Psalm 32:8 (KJV)**: "I will instruct thee and teach thee in the way which thou shalt go: I will guide thee with mine eye."

Reflection: In what areas of your life do you need to ask God for wisdom and guidance?

7. Forgiveness and Healing

When seeking forgiveness and healing, these scriptures remind us of God's mercy and His power to restore.

- **1 John 1:9 (KJV)**: "If we confess our sins, he is faithful... to forgive us our sins, and to cleanse us from all unrighteousness."
- **Jeremiah 17:14 (KJV)**: "Heal me, O LORD, and I shall be healed; save me, and I shall be saved."

Reflection: How can you open your heart to God's healing and let go of past guilt?

8. Purpose and Calling

These verses remind us that God has a plan and purpose for each of our lives.

- **Jeremiah 29:11 (KJV)**: "For I know the thoughts that I think toward you... to give you an expected end."
- **Romans 8:28 (KJV)**: "And we know that all things work together for good to them that love God."

Reflection: How are you living out your purpose, and where might God be leading you next?

9. Perseverance and Endurance

In times when it's hard to keep going, these scriptures call us to press forward, knowing that God is with us.

- **Galatians 6:9 (KJV)**: "Let us not be weary in well doing: for in due season we shall reap, if we faint not."
- **2 Timothy 4:7 (KJV)**: "I have fought a good fight, I have finished my course, I have kept the faith."

Reflection: How can you push through challenging moments with faith and endurance?

10. The Power of Prayer

These verses demonstrate the importance and effectiveness of prayer in all situations.

- **Matthew 7:7 (KJV)**: "Ask, and it shall be given you; seek, and ye shall find."
- **Ephesians 6:18 (KJV)**: "Praying always with all prayer and supplication in the Spirit... watching thereunto with all perseverance."

Reflection: How can you develop a deeper, more consistent prayer life?

11. Love and Relationships

The Bible teaches us that love is the foundation of all relationships, reflecting God's love for us.

- **1 Corinthians 13:4-7 (KJV)**: "Charity suffereth long, and is kind... beareth all things, believeth all things, hopeth all things."
- **John 13:34-35 (KJV)**: "A new commandment I give unto you, That ye love one another... by this shall all men know that ye are my disciples."

Reflection: How can you better show love and kindness in your relationships?

12. Hope in Times of Despair

When despair creeps in, these scriptures offer hope and the assurance of God's faithfulness.

- **Romans 15:13 (KJV)**: "Now the God of hope fill you with all joy and peace in believing, that ye may abound in hope."

- **Lamentations 3:22-23 (KJV):** "It is of the Lord's mercies that we are not consumed... They are new every morning: great is thy faithfulness."

Reflection: How can you hold onto hope, even in the darkest times?

13. Overcoming Fear and Doubt

In moments of fear or doubt, turn to these verses that remind us of God's power and faithfulness.

- **2 Timothy 1:7 (KJV):** "For God hath not given us the spirit of fear; but of power, and of love, and of a sound mind."
- **Isaiah 26:3 (KJV):** "Thou wilt keep him in perfect peace, whose mind is stayed on thee: because he trusteth in thee."

Reflection: What steps can you take to trust in God's strength rather than give in to fear and uncertainty?

14. Spiritual Growth and Maturity

These scriptures encourage continuous growth in faith and spiritual maturity.

- **Colossians 1:10 (KJV):** "That ye might walk worthy of the Lord unto all pleasing, being fruitful in every good work, and increasing in the knowledge of God."
- **Hebrews 5:14 (KJV):** "But strong meat belongeth to them that are of full age, even those who by reason of use have their senses exercised to discern both good and evil."

Reflection: In what ways can you deepen your walk with God and grow in spiritual wisdom?

15. Restoration and New Beginnings

God promises restoration and the opportunity for a new beginning, no matter how broken things may seem.

- **Joel 2:25 (KJV)**: "And I will restore to you the years that the locust hath eaten, the cankerworm, and the caterpiller, and the palmerworm."
- **Isaiah 43:19 (KJV)**: "Behold, I will do a new thing; now it shall spring forth; shall ye not know it?"

Reflection: How can you embrace the new beginning God offers in your life today?

16. The Power of God's Word

These scriptures highlight the life-changing power of God's Word and its ability to guide us.

- **Hebrews 4:12 (KJV)**: "For the word of God is quick, and powerful, and sharper than any twoedged sword."
- **Psalm 119:105 (KJV)**: "Thy word is a lamp unto my feet, and a light unto my path."

Reflection: How can you apply God's Word more consistently in your daily life?

17. Encouragement for Perseverance

These verses remind us to keep going, even in the face of hardship, knowing that our perseverance will be rewarded.

- **1 Corinthians 15:58 (KJV):** "Therefore, my beloved brethren, be ye stedfast, unmoveable, always abounding in the work of the Lord."
- **James 1:12 (KJV):** "Blessed is the man that endureth temptation: for when he is tried, he shall receive the crown of life."

Reflection: How does perseverance in your faith help you face daily challenges?

18. Gratitude and Praise

In all circumstances, we are called to give thanks and praise God for His goodness.

- **1 Thessalonians 5:18 (KJV):** "In every thing give thanks: for this is the will of God in Christ Jesus concerning you."
- **Psalm 100:4 (KJV):** "Enter into his gates with thanksgiving, and into his courts with praise: be thankful unto him, and bless his name."

Reflection: How can you cultivate a spirit of gratitude and praise, even in difficult times?

19. Strength in Weakness

God's strength is revealed in our moments of weakness, empowering us to overcome obstacles.

- **2 Corinthians 12:9 (KJV):** "And he said unto me, My grace is sufficient for thee: for my strength is made perfect in weakness."
- **Isaiah 40:31 (KJV):** "But they that wait upon the LORD shall renew their strength; they shall mount up with wings as eagles."

Reflection: How can you find strength in your weakness by relying on God's grace?

20. Spiritual Armor for Protection

God equips us with spiritual armor to stand firm against the challenges of life and the enemy's attacks.

- **Ephesians 6:11 (KJV):** "Put on the whole armour of God, that ye may be able to stand against the wiles of the devil."
- **Romans 13:12 (KJV):** "The night is far spent, the day is at hand: let us therefore cast off the works of darkness, and let us put on the armour of light."

Reflection: What areas of your life need God's protection and how can you actively put on His spiritual armor?

Closing Encouragement

Remember, the Word of God is living and active, and these verses are here to guide you through life's challenges. Keep them close to your heart, and never forget that no matter the struggle, God has already equipped you with the tools you need to overcome.

Stay Connected and Keep the Journey Going

Thank you for reading *Malt Liquor to Holy Water*. My journey doesn't stop here, and neither does yours have to.

If you're looking for more inspiration, practical advice, and faith-based guidance on overcoming addiction, visit my YouTube channel:

Quit Drinking With Bible

Explore powerful content rooted in scripture, just like the themes in this book. Learn how to take control of your life, one day at a time, with faith as your guide. Whether you're looking for a deeper connection to God or practical tools to quit drinking, my channel is here to help you on your path to freedom.

Music as the Soundtrack to This Book

Every story has a soundtrack, and mine is no different. The music that carried me through my transformation is now available to you. My album, **Malt Liquor to Holy Water**, is the official soundtrack to this book, capturing the highs, lows, and ultimate redemption of my journey.

You can find it on all major online music platforms:
- **Spotify**
- **iTUNES**
- **Amazon Music**
- **YouTube Music**
- And more...

Let the music remind you that no matter how deep the struggle, there's always a way up.

www.ingramcontent.com/pod-product-compliance
Lightning Source LLC
Chambersburg PA
CBHW021109130626
46554CB00002B/597